401
Practical
Adaptations
for Every Classroom

Beverley Holden Johns

401
Practical
Adaptations
for Every Classroom

CORWIN
A SAGE Company

For information:

Corwin
A SAGE Company
2455 Teller Road
Thousand Oaks, California 91320
(800) 233-9936
Fax: (800) 417-2466
www.corwin.com

SAGE Pvt. Ltd.
B 1/I 1 Mohan Cooperative
    Industrial Area
Mathura Road, New Delhi 110 044
India

SAGE Ltd.
1 Oliver's Yard
55 City Road
London EC1Y 1SP
United Kingdom

SAGE Asia-Pacific Pte. Ltd.
33 Pekin Street #02-01
Far East Square
Singapore 048763

Printed in the United States of America

Library of Congress Cataloging-in-Publication Data

Johns, Beverley H. (Beverley Holden)
401 practical adaptations for every classroom / Beverley Holden Johns.
    p. cm.
Includes bibliographical references and index.
ISBN 978-1-4129-8202-3 (pbk.)
    1. Children with disabilities—Education. 2. Remedial teaching. 3. Individualized instruction. I. Title. II. Title: Four hundred one practical adaptations for every classroom.

LC4015.J64 2011
371.9′043—dc22   2010031503

This book is printed on acid-free paper.

10   11   12   13   14   10   9   8   7   6   5   4   3   2   1

Acquisitions Editor:	Jessica Allan
Associate Editors:	Joanna Coelho and Allison Scott
Editorial Assistant:	Lisa Whitney
Production Editor:	Veronica Stapleton
Copy Editor:	Trey Thoelcke
Typesetter:	C&M Digitals (P) Ltd.
Proofreader:	Gretchen Treadwell
Indexer:	Molly Hall
Cover Designer:	Karine Hovsepian

Contents

Acknowledgments

Corwin gratefully acknowledges the contributions of the following reviewers.

Melody Aldrich
English Teacher
Poston Butte High School
San Tan Valley, AZ

Diane Callahan
Retired Science Teacher
Fairfield Middle School
West Chester, OH

Laurie Emery, EdD
Principal
Old Vail Middle School
Vail, AZ

Kristina Moody
Teacher
Gulfport High School
Gulfport, MS

Dana Stevens
Assistant Professor
Whitworth University School of Education
Spokane, WA

About the Author

 **Beverley Holden Johns** is a graduate of Catherine Spalding College in Louisville, Kentucky, and was awarded a fellowship for her graduate work at Southern Illinois University (SIU) in Carbondale, where she received an MS in special education. She has done postgraduate work at the University of Illinois, Western Illinois University, SIU, and Eastern Illinois University. Johns has thirty-nine years of experience working with students with learning disabilities (LD) and behavioral disorders (EBD) within the public schools. She supervised LD and EBD teachers in twenty-two school districts, was the founder and administrator of the Garrison Alternative School for students with severe EBD in Jacksonville, Illinois, and later served as coordinator for staff development for the Four Rivers Special Education District. She is now a learning and behavior consultant and an adjunct instructor for MacMurray College.

During her term as president of the International Association of Special Education (IASE) from 2006 until January 1, 2010, she chaired that organization's tenth Biennial Conference held June 10 to 14, 2007, in Hong Kong, and presided over the eleventh Biennial Conference in Alicante, Spain, in 2009. She presented the Inaugural Marden Lecture at the University of Hong Kong in January, 2006.

Johns is the lead author of *Reduction of School Violence: Alternatives to Suspension* (2009); *Techniques for Managing Verbally and Physically Aggressive Students* (2009); *Surviving Internal Politics Within the School* (2006); *Techniques for Managing a Safe School* (1997); *Effective Curriculum and Instruction for Students With Emotional/Behavioral Disorders* (2002); *Students With Disabilities and General Education: A Desktop Reference for School Personnel* (2007); *Getting Behavioral Interventions Right* (2005); *Preparing Test-Resistant Students for Assessments: A Staff Training Guide* (2007); *Ethical Dilemmas in Education* (2008); and *The Many Faces of Special Educators* (2010); She coauthored *Teacher's Reflective Calendar and Planning Journal* (Corwin, 2006); *Special Educator's Reflective Calendar and Planning Journal* (Corwin, 2009); and

Reaching Students With Diverse Disabilities (2008), as well as the seminal college LD textbook, the eleventh edition of *Learning Disabilities and Related Mild Disabilities* (with Janet Lerner, 2009). The twelfth edition will be published in 2011. She has written a workbook to accompany the video *The Paraprofessional's Guide to Managing Student Behavior* (2002) and more than forty education and special education articles.

She received the CEC Outstanding Leadership Award from the International Council for Exceptional Children (CEC) in 2000 and the Romaine P. Mackie Leadership Service Award in 2007. She was Jacksonville Woman of the Year in 1988, and cochaired the Business Education Partnership Committee and the Jacksonville Truancy Task Force. Johns is past president of the Council for Children With Behavioral Disorders (CCBD), the CEC Pioneers, and the Learning Disabilities Association (LDA) of Illinois and has served as the national state presidents' representative on the board of LDA of America and chair of governmental relations for several national and state organizations. She has presented workshops across the United States and Canada as well as in San Juan, Puerto Rico; Sydney, Australia (keynote); Warsaw and Wroclaw, Poland; Hong Kong, China; Lima, Peru; and Riga, Latvia.

Johns is listed in *Who's Who in America, Who's Who of American Women, Who's Who in American Education,* and *Who's Who Among America's Teachers* and has chaired the Illinois Special Education Coalition (ISELA), whose membership includes thirteen statewide organizations, for thirty years.

1

Introduction to Adaptations

Why the Need and Important Considerations

What can I do to meet the diverse needs of the students in my class-room? How can I accommodate Julian's needs and still meet the needs of my twenty-five other students? How can I provide adaptations that don't require an inordinate amount of my time? How can I provide adaptations that don't cost a lot of money?

Are you looking for practical answers to these questions? If so, this book is for you. Loaded with practical ideas, this book is designed to meet your needs. You have taken the first step to making your classroom a more user-friendly place for your students with special needs.

The number of students with special needs in general education class-rooms is increasing, along with the expansion of the inclusion movement. This calls for development of effective adaptations, useful modifications, and needed accommodations for students with special needs. Additionally, the push to include most students in our assessment system has brought to the forefront the need for accommodations in assessment. To be suc-cessful in the general education curriculum, students with special needs require support through adaptations.

You may hear colleagues say, "It's not my job to accommodate students with special needs—if I had wanted to work with students with special needs I'd have gone into special education." While such an attitude is problematic in today's classrooms because of the diverse needs of the children, we all must be cognizant of the needs of the classroom teacher. Classroom teachers are bombarded with expectations from school and society. They are expected to work with a large group of students—some classrooms may have forty students in them. Teachers feel a tremendous sense of pressure because of our focus on high-stakes testing. The scores of the students may be published in the newspaper, and often teachers are blamed for low test scores even when they do not have control over all the variables influencing the children within their classroom.

Teachers at the secondary level are content specialists and are expected to cover a specific amount of material by given dates. All teachers feel the pressure to teach to standards, even when they question whether all of their students are prepared for those standards. Students in any given classroom read at different levels, may have attendance problems, and may come with the emotional baggage of not liking school.

At the same time, we expect teachers to work with more diverse students, even though many of them have had only one special education class during their training programs.

Because of the many challenges classroom teachers face, we must all be reasonable in the adaptations that we expect them to make. It is unreasonable to expect a classroom teacher to spend three hours a day recording a reading book for a student or for a general education teacher to work with an individual for two hours during the school day—what happens to the other students during that time?

Classroom teachers must be active participants in discussions about what adaptations are reasonable to make within the classroom and what adaptations will require assistance to make. I remember participating in an Individualized Education Program (IEP) for a high school student. All of the high school teachers were present and the discussion focused on whether a word bank might be appropriate for a student during testing. One of the teachers had a blank look and asked, "What is a word bank?" I was delighted that he spoke up and admitted he did not know what it was.

Many teachers are willing to make accommodations but need assistance to make them. The purpose of this book is to give teachers an array of adaptations that are not labor intensive for their students and will make teaching easier. A teacher may discover that an adaptation for one student works for other students as well.

This chapter sets the stage for the remainder of this book. It outlines the meaning of the terms *adaptations, accommodations,* and *modifications.* It also includes the legal basis for adaptations. It reviews the cautions in the use of adaptations, discusses the importance of record keeping, and provides helpful tips for collaboration.

DEFINITIONS OF TERMS

You may hear people use the terms *adaptations, accommodations,* and *modifications* interchangeably; however, these terms are different. The following graphic and definitions will help you distinguish among the terms.

Figure 1.1

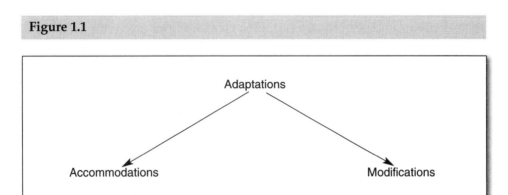

Adaptations. Consider this an umbrella term that encompasses all modifications and accommodations. Practical adaptations are strategies to support students with special needs and to improve their learning.

Modifications. This term involves changes in the general education curriculum, course content, teaching strategies, manner of presentation, or timing. For example, a student could be assigned fewer spelling words to memorize or be given an easier history text to read. The teacher might use materials that provide a high level of interest for older students but that use lower vocabulary than typical grade level materials. The teacher also might use off-grade level material for some students. That is, the student might be in the sixth grade but with math skills at a third-grade level, so the teacher opts to include third-grade math problems. When you modify content or instruction, you are monkeying with the content. A picture of a monkey may help you remember that a modification changes or monkeys with the content.

Accommodations. These are applied to the curriculum and instruction and assessment. Accommodations do not change the content but rather provide "the extension ladder" for students to get where they need to be. For example, if I need to change a fluorescent lightbulb in a ceiling that is eight feet tall but I am only a little over five feet tall, I will need a ladder to change the lightbulb. I have the skills—I am "otherwise qualified" to do this job—but I must use a ladder to get me to where I need to be to change the lightbulb. Glasses and hearing aids are accommodations. A wheelchair is an accommodation for a person who cannot walk. Extended time to take a test is a frequently requested accommodation. Another example of an accommodation is permitting a student with a fine-motor disability to use a word processor to take a writing test.

Accommodations in assessment should match the accommodations in instruction. For example, if a student is to be provided with a calculator for a specific math assessment, that student should be taught how to operate the calculator and should use it during classroom instruction.

Examples of accommodations might include a large print book for a student who has a visual impairment or a student with a learning disability who has difficulty tracking the text. A pencil grip, a word processor for writing, or being able to write on the test booklet rather than having to put the answers on a bubble sheet are also accommodations. There are quite a lot of accommodations, which may or may not be appropriate for the student, and this book discusses many of them.

WHY THE NEED FOR ACCOMMODATIONS: WHAT THE LAW SAYS

Several laws govern the appropriate use of accommodations and modifications for students with special needs. These laws serve to protect students and their families, as well as to provide guidance to all educators on implementation of the provision of services for students with disabilities. It is critical that all educators understand the basic requirements of these laws.

Individuals With Disabilities Education Act (IDEA)

In 1997's IDEA, for the first time, the general education teacher was required to participate in the Individualized Education Program process. Teachers' organizations had voiced serious concerns that, with the movement toward inclusion, they were being expected to provide significant services and accommodations for students with disabilities within their classroom yet were not involved in the decision-making process. There was also an addition in the focus of the IEP process. Previously the IEP team addressed the needs of the student alone. With IDEA, language was added to support school personnel. Consequently, if teachers state, within the IEP process, that they need additional training to meet the needs of the student, then the training must be addressed within the IEP process (Johns, 1998).

The subsequent reauthorization of the act (still known as IDEA) in 2004 retained these important revisions.

Thus, the IEP team is charged with examining the needs of the student, planning goals, and then determining how and where those goals can be met. It is critical for the IEP team to consider the whole range of student needs. Students who have a disability that results in an adverse effect on educational performance require specialized instruction to meet those needs. They also require sufficient accommodations in assessment and instruction. They may require specific modifications to the general curriculum. They also may require related services coordinated with their special education program and placement. It is the IEP team that makes these decisions and the general education teacher is an integral part of that process.

IDEA also requires that students are educated in the least restrictive environment—that means that students are educated to the maximum extent appropriate with their nondisabled peers. It doesn't mean that all students are educated within the general education classroom, but it means that children with disabilities are educated as appropriate with their peers. The IEP team determines placement.

No Child Left Behind

School personnel struggle to meet the requirements of No Child Left Behind (NCLB) Act of 2001, which looks at all students and at what level they achieve as compared to their grade level peers, while at the same time educators must also address the individual needs of the student as the cornerstone of the IDEA-2004. NCLB focuses on accountability for results for all students. Students must take a state-determined assessment, and then each state's department of education compiles the results of the tests. Each state must report the information back to the school district, while also reporting the school and district results to the public via the newspaper and Internet. All students must make adequate yearly progress (AYP) in reading, math, and science. Scores are disaggregated for specific groups of students—students with disabilities may be a disaggregated group of students, depending on the number of students that the state has determined as the minimum size of a disaggregated group. Data is disaggregated for students by poverty levels, race ethnicities, disabilities, and English Language Learners (U.S. Department of Education, 2002).

For students with disabilities, the IEP team determines whether the student takes the state assessment with or without accommodations. If the student takes the test with accommodations, the IEP team determines the specific accommodations that should mirror the accommodations made within instruction. The IEP team may determine that the student can take one part of the test without accommodations but for another part of the test the student does need accommodations. The student may be able to take the math test with no accommodations but needs to be accommodated when taking the reading test. No more than 1 percent of all students with the most significant cognitive disabilities may take an alternate assessment based on alternate achievement standards. An additional 2 percent may be eligible to take an alternate assessment based on modified academic achievement standards. All of these decisions are made by the IEP team.

Section 504 of the Rehabilitation Act of 1973

Section 504 of the Rehabilitation Act of 1973 prohibits discrimination on the basis of a disability. Section 504 also provides reasonable accommodations to students with disabilities and those accommodations are to be determined within the scope of a Section 504 accommodation plan for the student who has a disability but may not be eligible for special education. A few examples of accommodations that might be made for a student who requires a 504 plan but is not in special education might include periodic bathroom breaks for a student with diabetes, dietary requirements for a student with specific allergies, or removal of barriers for a student who uses a wheelchair.

The definition of a disability was changed as a result of the reauthorization of the Americans with Disabilities Act (ADA). The ADA Amendments Act of 2008 amended the definition of a disability. The term *disability* means a physical or mental impairment that substantially limits one or more major life activities of the individual. Major life activities include but are not limited to caring for oneself, performing manual tasks, seeing, hearing, eating, sleeping, walking, standing, lifting, bending, speaking, breathing, learning, reading, concentrating, thinking, communicating, and working. An individual meets the requirements of having an impairment if the individual establishes that he or she has been subjected to an action because of an actual or perceived physical or mental impairment, whether or not the impairment limits or is perceived to limit a major life activity. The determination of whether an impairment substantially limits a major life activity is made without regard to the ameliorative effects of mitigating measures such as medication, medical supplies, equipment, or appliances including low-vision devices, prosthetics, hearing aids, and cochlear implants. It does not include the effects of ordinary eyeglasses or contact lenses (ADA Amendments Act of 2008).

Under Section 504, an appropriate education means an education comparable to the education of other students without disabilities, unlike IDEA, which defines an appropriate education as one that meets the individualized needs of the student.

A student with a disability may be eligible for the provisions of Section 504, yet not eligible for services under the IDEA. For a student to be eligible for services under IDEA, the student must exhibit a disability that results in an adverse effect on educational performance. First, the evaluation team determines whether there is a disability. If a disability is determined to exist, then the team determines whether it has an adverse effect on educational performance. If there is no adverse effect, then the student may need accommodations for his or her disability and will require an accommodation plan under Section 504. If an adverse effect exists, then the student would be eligible for special education and need an IEP.

Doe v. Withers

In the case of *Doe v. Withers*, 20 IDELR 422 (West Va. Circuit Court, 1993), the court ruled against a history teacher for failure to make the necessary accommodations for the student. The teacher clearly knew that the accommodations were to be made and refused to allow the student to have tests read orally to him. The principal attempted to persuade the history teacher to make the accommodations but the teacher would not do so. The state court in West Virginia ordered the history teacher to pay a judgment of $5,000 in actual damages, plus $10,000 in punitive damages, for failure to administer the tests to the student orally (Zirkel, 1994).

CAUTIONS IN THE USE OF ACCOMMODATIONS

Accommodations are not an instructional substitute

In schools today, we all work hard to ensure that students receive the accommodations that they need to be successful in both assessment and instruction. However, all educators also must make sure that the student with a disability who is in special education also receives the specialized instruction that the student needs and that specialized instruction is individually tailored to meet that student's needs.

As an example, Jessica may be in sixth grade but reads at a second-grade level. When Jessica is in her general education classes, it is critical that she receive accommodations for her reading problem—her books may be on tape, someone may be reading the text to her, or her materials may be digitized. However, at the same time, Jessica must be taught how to read in a way that is individually tailored for her. She must receive specialized instruction by a special educator. Accommodations are not enough for Jessica.

In another example, students often are given the accommodation of extended timelines for taking tests or completing assignments. However, extended timelines may not be beneficial to a student who has not been taught how to manage his or her time.

Accommodations are not giveaways

I once heard a general education teacher say that she would not allow her students to take a test in the special education room. When I asked her why, she replied that she was afraid the special education teacher would give the student the answers to the questions. I explained that the job of the individual who administers the accommodation is not to provide the the answer; it is to read the question to the student so the student can offer an answer. Accommodations were never designed to give away answers to students, and anyone who administers specific accommodations must be very careful that they do not give the students clues that should not be given. They are not to answer the question for the student, but to simply administer the test with the needed accommodation. They must be careful even that voice inflection does not give away an answer. If the student requires a scribe (the student verbally relays the answer and the individual accommodating writes down exactly what the student says), the adult must not write down what he or she wanted the student to say. Those who administer accommodations should have extensive training in not giving answers to students.

Accommodations must address the preferences of the students

The preference of the student for a specific accommodation must be strongly considered. Some years ago, I participated in an IEP for a secondary student who had a processing deficit in the area of auditory skills—specifically in auditory memory. He was failing one of his classes because the teacher primarily used the lecture method. We were discussing the possibility that the student might use a tape recorder in the class so he could take it home and listen to the lecture more than once. The student quickly spoke up: "I hate using tape recorders." It was back to the drawing board for the IEP team. After all, an accommodation is designed to help a student—not force that student to use an unwanted tool.

In another common example that I have seen, the school provides assignment notebooks for all the students. Personnel find that some students respond well to that while other students are conveniently losing the notebook. Personnel try to figure out why those students are not using a tool that was designed to help them. It may be that the assignment notebook is a weekly guide for students and they are overwhelmed by seeing the whole week at once. The notebook just isn't a match for the student. Many of us have different types of planners—some people use a day at a glance, others utilize a weekly planner, some individuals want to see the whole month at a time, and some adults prefer an electronic calendar. I prefer to see the whole month at one time and know what I have to do over the month—if you told me I could no longer use a monthly planner, I would probably rebel, because that is not my preference.

You may ask how you can learn about the preferences of your students. Many of them will tell us. Others don't know enough about various types of accommodations to tell us. We must expose our students to a variety of types of accommodations and let them experience those accommodations and see what works best for them. Not too long ago, I spilled coffee all over my computer and bid my computer goodbye. I was upset by what I had done and was sharing my sad story to a friend; she immediately told me about an excellent accommodation I could use—it was a slip that would go over the keyboard and protect it while still allowing me to type. She even told me where I could order one and I went right home and did so. Initially excited to put it on my new laptop, I quickly discovered I hated the feel of it and couldn't stand to use it. So much for that accommodation—I instead realized that it would be better if I just made sure I didn't have coffee or any other liquid anywhere close to my computer.

I was working with a student with a learning disability who required accommodations under Section 504 of the Rehabilitation Act. Specifically, tests were to be read to her. At the beginning of the year, I met with her to get to know her better. I specifically asked her whether she would like a proctor to read any tests to her or whether she preferred that I read the test questions into a tape recorder and then she could take the test in a private room where she could listen to the questions as many times as she needed. She preferred the second option because she was not comfortable with having the test read to her by someone she didn't know.

ACCURATE RECORD KEEPING: IF IT ISN'T WRITTEN DOWN, IT WASN'T DONE

Accommodations and modifications for students who are in special education are determined by the IEP team and must be delineated in that document. Accommodations for students who are eligible under Section 504 of the Rehabilitation Act of 1973 are determined via the Section 504 accommodation plan. Accommodations should be thoroughly discussed and documented in the IEP or 504 plan. It is helpful also to document the results of the use of accommodations and the effectiveness of specific accommodations. As an example, the student's previous IEP may have noted that the student was in need of extended timelines for assessments. However, when the teacher recently observed the student in a testing situation, she noted that he could get the assignment done within the regular timeline. The teacher will want to come prepared to discuss whether extended timelines should be continued.

I can remember attending one IEP meeting in which we had a good discussion of the necessary accommodations for a student. We determined as a group the needed accommodations, but I noticed that the person writing the IEP was not recording any of the information. When we had a break, I told her what I had noticed. She replied, "Oh, there isn't any need—we make those accommodations for anyone in this school district." I explained nicely that if the student moved, the IEP would go with her and that the receiving school district would have no way of knowing what the child needed. The IEP is a portable document. When a student moves to a new school district, personnel there should be able to review the IEP and determine the needs of the student.

ONE SIZE DOES NOT FIT ALL

Many school districts employ accommodation checklists for IEPs and some do the same for the Section 504 accommodation plan. Checklists are acceptable if they reflect the needs of the individual child. However, when accommodation plans are included in the IEP and school personnel check all of the accommodations (just in case the student may need them) they are not really considering the individual needs of the student. The accommodations discussion within the IEP should be meaningful for the needs of the child. Accommodations should be designed specific to the types of disabilities. The appropriateness of the accommodation has been noted in research as interacting with the specific nature of the disability of the student (Fletcher et al., 2009). Through assessment and observation, both the general and special education teacher should come to the IEP prepared to discuss what needs the student has and how those needs can be met.

THE IMPORTANCE OF COLLABORATION IN PLANNING APPROPRIATE ADAPTATIONS

The process of collaboration is based on the belief that individuals working together bring their own expertise to the table and each party can learn from and benefit from each other's time and talent. Successful collaborators recognize the strengths of each of the parties and come to the table with an open mind and a clear focus that the purpose of the collaboration is to help the student succeed.

Collaboration as a delivery system has increased in popularity, especially since 1990. Prior to that time, special educators and regular educators were generally expected to deal on their own with the problems that they faced within their respective classrooms. Those who asked for help were perceived as unable to do their job and such requests may have then been rejected by their supervisors or peers (Kampwirth, 2003).

Times have changed. The IEP is a team process, and teacher assistance teams or student support teams are more common in schools. Educators are realizing that they do not have all the answers, that two heads are better than one. Such role changes indicate a trend in society in general. In contrast to earlier times when the majority of workers toiled in isolation on assembly lines, the majority of jobs available today require much interaction with fellow workers and customers. We are all bombarded with so much information that we cannot have all the answers to all of the problems. We must work actively with our colleagues. We want our students to grow up and work collaboratively in teams in the workplace. Educators are role models, so it is critical that students see their teachers working together in the spirit of teamwork.

The classroom teacher has the expertise in the area of the general curriculum and how typical children learn. The classroom teacher has realistic expectations of what may be accomplished in a classroom of twenty-five to thirty students. The special educator has knowledge about specialized interventions and how to accommodate and modify instruction and assessment. When they come together, they can brainstorm effective strategies for students.

When classroom teachers collaborate with families, they share with the parents the progress the student has made within the classroom and the areas of concern that might exist. The parents bring their expertise of knowing the strengths, weaknesses, and interests of their child. Webster-Stratton and Reid (2002) summarized the research literature on the key features of effective parent programs. Those that are collaborative result in more parental engagement.

Strategies for Effective Collaboration

- **Be a good listener.** The ability to "listen" may be 80 percent of the special and general education teachers' role as a good collaborator (DeBoer, 1986, 1995).
- **Be realistic.** When collaborating with a fellow teacher, a parent, or a related services provider such as a social worker or psychologist, teachers should be realistic in what they expect these colleagues to do and recognize their time or money available, or other challenges they face.
- **Be empathetic.** Teachers must make every effort to put themselves in the other person's place and see the issue from the other perspective. Active listening can help in understanding the feelings of coworkers and better understanding the other person's needs.
- **Be positive and upbeat.** It is important that educators be positive and upbeat and provide a sense of hope to those with whom they collaborate. If the classroom teacher is feeling down or feeling like a failure because the special needs of a student are not being met, the other individual should encourage and support the teacher in his or her everyday work.
- **Be dependable.** It is important for members of the team to have confidence in other members. If you say you will do some task, do it in a timely fashion. Otherwise another member of the team may lose confidence in you.
- **Be in tune to the needs of others.** All behavior is a form of communication. Teachers may be telling others what their needs are through their behavior. For example, a teacher may be resistant to working with a particular student and communicate that resistance through a variety of behaviors, such as exhibiting attention, power, revenge, and inadequacy (Dreikurs, 1964). For example, the teacher might appear to be too busy to work with the special educator to meet the needs of the student, when the teacher is really fearful that he or she won't be successful with the student. The teacher might complain often about the size of classes as a way to say that she or he doesn't want the special education student within the classroom, when in fact the teacher is saying he or she needs more assistance in working with the student. The teacher might say, "I don't have time to do this," when in fact the teacher is really saying he or she needs help to make the accommodation.

I have always believed that all educators must be lifelong learners—we never have all the answers to the challenges that we face in today's schools. We read and study, attend professional development, and work together with our colleagues. Sometimes we are too close to a situation and need to work together with others to get a fresh perspective about a situation. We may think we have tried everything but then a colleague comes up with an idea we hadn't considered. The beauty of collaboration is that we learn from each other.

Summary: Just 3×5 It

I can still remember a colleague, who wanted to let me know that she didn't want a long explanation of something, telling me to "Just 3×5 it." She only wanted a brief summary of the key points. I sometimes like to make 3×5 review cards for my students as a handy reference for them to use to remember key points. They can then carry the cards around with them.

All of the chapter summaries provide 3×5 review cards.

The summary of this chapter, and all subsequent chapters, is designed to give you the key points from the chapter and a quick review of what you have learned.

1. *Adaptation* is the umbrella term used to describe both accommodations and modifications within the classroom. Accommodations don't change the content. Modifications do change the content.

2. Individuals with Disabilities Education Act (IDEA) is the special education law that protects the individual rights of children with disabilities who are in need of specially designed instruction based on their needs.

3. No Child Left Behind (NCLB) focuses on assessment and accountability, and it also stresses testing of students at given grade levels.

4. Section 504 of the Rehabilitation Act of 1973 prohibits discrimination against any individual with a disability. The Americans with Disabilities Act (ADA) provides protections to individuals throughout their lifetimes in workplace and society.

5. *Doe v. Withers* was a case that dealt with a classroom teacher's refusal to make accommodations for a student with a learning disability.

6. Cautions in the use of accommodations that educators should monitor to determine their appropriate use include that accommodations are not instructional substitutes nor giveaways, and that they should be individualized and based on the preferences of students.

7. Accurate record keeping and documentation about the effectiveness of accommodations is critical.

8. Collaboration provides us with an important avenue to gain expertise about interventions from other educators and families.

2

Adaptations on a Shoestring Budget

Has your classroom budget been cut? Do you have limited resources to purchase materials? Most educators have faced these dilemmas and find themselves unable to purchase expensive materials for their classroom. Adaptations for students do not have to cost a lot of money. This chapter focuses on those materials that you can purchase for your classroom that don't cost a lot—and at the same time you can make a variety of adaptations for your students. Adaptations provided here require four cheap items (listed below) that can be purchased at dollar stores, ordered from a discount catalogue, or purchased at an office store prior to the beginning of the school year, when there are back-to-school sales and discounts for teachers. I like to scout dollar stores for items all year long and always take advantage of the back-to-school sales to stock up on items I will need throughout the year.

Many of the adaptations described in this chapter are not only appropriate for students with special needs but for other students as well as we work to challenge and motivate them. These adaptations can be varied according to the age of the student. I have found them to be effective for very young children through postsecondary schooling.

Here is everything you will need to make the adaptations in this chapter.

- File folders
- Index cards
- Sticky notes
- Red rubber balls or beach balls

LOW-COST ADAPTATIONS

File Folders

File folders can have multiple uses for adaptations within the classroom. Many students feel overwhelmed by too much material on a page and they can't focus on all of the material at one time. Some children become upset by too many math problems on a page, for instance. Some may be easily distracted and can't focus on one item. File folders can resolve some of those problems.

- An easy adaptation is made for an overwhelmed child when a teacher takes a standard file folder and cuts the front cover into four or five strips without disconnecting the strips from the folder. The teacher can then put a worksheet or reading assignment into the file folder. Then the student, rather than looking at the entire worksheet at one time, can flip over each strip individually so only the part on which she or he is working is visible. These file folders can also serve as a type of ruler guide for a child who has difficulty keeping his or her place or staying on a line.
- For students who have difficulty writing within a given set of margins and run out of space at the end of the line, the teacher can take a file folder and cut out a picture frame on the front. The teacher then puts the child's writing paper in the file folder and the student can write within the margins because the cutout has provided a boundary.
- For students who forget to put their names on their paper, a teacher can cut out a box on the file folder for the student's name to appear. Beside the box, *Name* can be marked as a friendly reminder. The student's worksheet is then placed inside the file folder and the student is prompted by the file folder to write his or her name.
- The teacher can purchase a number of four-by-four-inch stickers from a dollar store that have states and capitals, math fact tables, punctuation marks, money designations, and more. I like to provide students with file folders for various subjects and then put one of the stickers on the front of the appropriate folder. For example, the math folder might have the math facts sticker as a reminder to the student.
- The teacher can cut out a given number of boxes on the front cover of a file folder for students who have difficulty writing their spelling words or keeping their math problems within a given space. The cutouts can be as large as the teacher believes the student will need to do a math problem or write a spelling word.
- For students who have difficulty writing a short essay, the teacher can cut the file folder's front cover into four strips, with each strip marked as follows: the top strip includes a prompt to write a topic

sentence. The next strip cues the student to write a supporting idea. The following strip is marked so the student knows to write another supporting idea. The bottom strip prompts the student to write a conclusion. When a blank writing sheet is placed inside, the file folder guides the student to complete an essay.

- To assist students who are sometimes overwhelmed at the thought of doing a book report, the teacher can likewise cut the front of a file folder into strips. The first strip prompts the student to write a name and the book or story title. Then the student flips over the second strip, which offers space to write about the main characters. The third strip is for the main problem in the story, and the following strip is for the story outcome. The last strip can be a brief list of main events. The strips can be varied according to the teacher's requirements for a book or story report.
- A teacher shared with me that he adapted a file folder for current events. He had students review the newspaper and write a short paragraph about each of three important stories. As a prompt for his students, he cut a file folder's front cover into three strips, in the same vein as the adaptations described previously.
- Teachers who are having difficulty getting students to proofread their own work can make a proofreading checklist and glue it to the front of the appropriate subject's file folder. Or, if students have been taught a test-taking strategy, the strategy can be printed on the front of a folder with the test inside.

These are just a few ideas to stimulate your thought process about how you can use a file folder as an adaptation. Put on your creative thinking cap and I bet you can come up with many more ideas.

Index Cards

Many of us use index cards for a variety of purposes. We may write ourselves notes for studying or use them as bookmarks with key ideas. We also may use index cards to help us keep our places when we read. These cards are helpful to us and also provide very inexpensive tools for adaptations for our students.

- As I recommended in the section on file folders, a teacher can cut a hole in an index card for those students who may have difficulty focusing on individual words. The index card covers up the rest of the words when placed over the reading material. The student can progress by moving the card left to right.
- Research by Heward (1996) shows us that there will be a decrease in behavior problems and an increase in engagement of students when response cards are used. Rather than the teacher asking a question

and those students who know the answer raising their hands, when the teacher asks a question, all students write an answer on their index card, and then hold up the card with their answer. This engages all students.

- I was talking to an individual who was diagnosed with ADHD when she was working on her PhD. She had managed to do very well in school in grasping concepts and on tests because she had learned to take her notes in class on index cards. She would then go home and take out the index cards, pacing back and forth while studying them. She found pacing with the cards helped her to remember what she needed to know. Some students may prefer to take notes on index cards so that they can pace while studying or can shuffle the cards to study.

- Index cards can be used as vocabulary cards. Students can be given a supply of index cards and a holder in which to put them. On one side of each card, students should write a vocabulary word that they are trying to learn. On the other side, they can add a drawing to help them remember the word.

- It may help students in the organization of their writing to use note cards to make an outline as illustrated in Figure 2.1. This can then guide the student in writing an essay on a topic (Lapsansky, 1991).

Figure 2.1

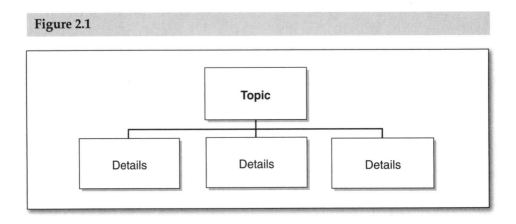

- When studying vocabulary words, math facts, or key social studies or science facts, the teacher can put key words or facts on a set of cards. The meanings or the answers can be put on other cards. I call this activity *dominoes* when I use it with my students. The teacher shuffles the cards and disseminates them to the students, who then have to find the student with the match to their card. This is not only a good review for the words or facts, but also gets the students up and moving. (I have found that this activity is a good way to get students into pairs. Another variation is to put groups of four words that go together to create a group of four.)

- For a student to match vocabulary words with definitions, or math facts, a teacher can make a deck of cards for the student or have the student create one. Shuffle the cards, put them facedown, and then have the student try to match the appropriate word with the definition or the math fact with the correct answer by revealing one card at a time.

Sticky Notes

We all probably use sticky notes throughout the day—we may write lists on them or mark significant spots in books. They can be put to good use as a classroom adaptation as well. Sticky notes come in a variety of sizes and shapes for varied uses.

- Students can learn to mark significant sections in their textbooks so they know where to look to find something. Sticky notes are available that have question marks and exclamation points on them. I like to use those to have students read a chapter and put question marks where they need further explanation from me as the teacher. Then I have them put an exclamation point on the critical information that they read.
- I like to do a textbook scavenger hunt at the beginning of the year for social studies texts or another content area text. I request that students locate certain sections of their book—the table of contents, the index, the glossary, certain charts, or other resources in the book. I give each student a supply of small sticky notes and they are to find the page where the information is located and mark the page(s) with a sticky note.
- I was working with a teacher who had a student with Asperger syndrome in her classroom. He would become agitated and begin to get hyperactive since he was in a large math class. The teacher knew it was important that she not single him out and call attention to his inappropriate behavior. We worked out a system in which she would explain to him that he and the teacher had a private signal. When he became overly active, she would place a small sticky note on her ink pen and move around the room, making sure the student saw her. That was the signal that it was time for him to quiet down. The teacher didn't need to say anything and it was an excellent visual strategy. Not to mention the fact that the student felt like he had a special relationship with the teacher because they had a private signal.
- Some older students do not like receiving praise in front of their peers. For those students, I keep a supply of sticky notes on my desk and when I see a student acting appropriately or helping another student or working hard on an assignment, I write a quick note saying something like, "Thanks for working on that" or "I appreciate you helping Joe."

- Some students are embarrassed to ask a question in front of the group. To allow them to ask a question, I establish a "parking lot." I place a picture of a big school bus on the wall and give students a supply of sticky notes. If they have a question, they can feel free to park their question on the parking lot, and during breaks I check it and make sure I answer the questions.
- When brainstorming ideas or if I want an anonymous opinion about a specific topic, I relate to the students what I am looking for. I put a poster up on the wall. Students write their idea or opinion on a sticky note and post it anonymously on the wall. We can then take a tally of the ideas or opinions.
- For older students, whom I may be teaching for only one period a day, I write the activities for the session on large sticky notes in the order of what we will do. I then post those on the board. As we complete an activity, I remove the sticky note from the board so the students can visually see what we have accomplished.

RED RUBBER BALLS (OR BEACH BALLS)

I still remember the day when a former custodian at my school said, "How many more of these red rubber balls are we going to have in this school building?" I loved using the red rubber ball—about fourteen inches in diameter, though the size can vary—for a variety of activities, as did many of my colleagues who had seen me use the activities. Here are just a few adaptations that you can use with the ball.

- When originally doing these activities, I would purchase a ball (preferably red). All over the ball, I would write questions that were a review of an activity that we had done. The students just loved the idea. I would break the students into teams. I would throw the ball. The student who caught the ball had to read the question under her or his left thumb. The student who caught the ball did not have to answer the question—the other team members had to do so. Otherwise no student would ever want to catch the ball (Johns, Crowley, & Guetzloe, 2002). I recently ran into a high school chemistry teacher who had attended a workshop I had done on adaptations—she was excited to tell me that she used the ball to help her students review chemistry formulas. They loved it and it really helped them to remember and made chemistry fun. Another grandma friend of mine made one for her four-year-old grandson—he likes to play catch so she made a ball with numbers on it and uses the ball to play catch while teaching him his numbers.

- You can also use the activity as an alternative to a worksheet for an individual child. As an example, the ball has many math problems at the appropriate level for the student. The student throws the ball up in the air and wherever his or her left thumb lands, the student writes down the problem on a piece of paper and then answers the problem. The teacher can request that the child answer a certain number of different problems—like ten of them. You can purchase some premade balls for a variety of purposes—algebraic equations, money—but I find it much cheaper to make my own. Also, I can customize the balls when I make my own.

- For children with autism or Asperger syndrome who have great interests in specific characters like Dora the Explorer, Nemo, Superman, or others, go to a dollar store and find a ball with the character on it. Then with a permanent marker, write math problems or reading words on that ball. Children will be motivated to do the academic subject.

- The advantage of using a beach ball is that you can deflate it for reduced storage space. You can purchase a beach ball that is a world globe—this is great for reviewing names of countries and their locations. A large beach ball also may be used as a cushion for a student. Inflate a beach ball slightly and a student can then sit on it—it allows the student to wiggle around more in the chair.

- Purchase a happy face ball and make it into a stress reducing ball. On the ball, write with a permanent marker various activities that are stress reducing, such as plaster a smile on your face, rub some lotion on your hands, think of something that makes you happy, say, "I am a great person." What I then like to do is to throw the ball around the room to each student before the class takes a test. This relieves some of their stress.

- A ball can be used as an icebreaker as well. Write a variety of questions on the ball—what is your favorite TV show, what is your favorite book, who is your hero, what is your favorite food. Throw the ball to students and have them answer the questions.

- You can use the ball as a way for the child to find out what activity to do as a follow up to a lesson. For instance, if you have been studying Abraham Lincoln, you can write on the ball a variety of activities that the student can do—draw a picture of Lincoln, write a poem about him, do a book report about him, make a game including key facts about Lincoln. Toss the ball to each student and wherever the left-hand thumb lands is the activity to do next.

- Students can fill their own red rubber balls with questions when they are studying for a test. You can pair the students so they can throw the ball back and forth as a review.

Summary: Just 3×5 It

1. File folders can be used to reduce the amount of work a student sees at one time, to provide friendly reminders, and to provide guidance for writing paragraphs and book reports.

2. Index cards can be used as windows for reading, response cards, a memory game, a note-taking device, and study guides, as well as to assist in organizing for a writing activity.

3. A variation of the game of dominoes is a great way to study facts and provide the opportunity for movement.

4. Sticky notes can be used to mark specific sections of the textbook.

5. Sticky notes can be used for signaling, questions, praise notes, and for posting a schedule.

6. Red rubber balls or beach balls can be used individually as an alternative to a worksheet, or students can create their own review balls.

7. Red rubber balls or beach balls can be used as a team game for review, a stress reducer, an icebreaker, or a choice activity.

8. A beach ball, partially inflated, can be used as a seat cushion.

3

Lecture Adaptations

In one of my classes, I always knew that I had lectured too long when one of my students with ADHD started twirling her hair. That was my cue that I needed to stop and do an activity with my students. I had talked too much; she was tuning me out and needed some movement. So she twirled her hair.

Some teachers think that the primary way to impart knowledge is through the teacher-directed lecture. However, attending and listening to lectures are very difficult for students with special needs. Students with ADHD have difficulty paying attention, students with auditory memory problems have difficulty remembering what the teacher has said, and students with auditory processing deficits have difficulty processing the information that the teacher conveys.

Many students without special needs find themselves daydreaming and zoning out of the lecture. Their minds are a lot of other places, rather than in the classroom. Most students are expected to take notes, but as a colleague once stated, their notes look like Swiss cheese. While students are trying to take notes, the teacher has moved on to the next part of the lecture. Some students find the information boring and are not interested in listening to what is being imparted.

Classroom teachers also find themselves with an increasing population of students who may be suffering from depression or anxiety disorders. Depression can be associated with problems in concentration and academic performance, and these students may feel overwhelmed by schoolwork. Children with anxiety may find it very difficult to attend during school activities (Brentar, 2008).

It has been found that students with emotional or behavioral disorders exhibit serious deficits across all academic subjects. They may perform up to two grade levels behind while in elementary school, and by the time these students reach high school they may be performing up to three and a half grade levels below normally developing students (Griffith Trout, Hagaman, & Harper, 2008). Dual deficits of learning and behavior problems make it very difficult for teachers to provide effective instruction (Sutherland, Lewis-Palmer, Stichter, & Morgan, 2008). All of these challenges faced by students result also in challenges to teachers in meeting their needs.

While more teachers are accompanying their lectures with PowerPoint slides, this is not enough for many students who need even more active participation.

It is critical that the teacher adapt lectures to promote maximum engagement for students who have difficulty paying attention. This chapter provides several adaptations for lectures.

IDEAS FOR LECTURE ADAPTATIONS

- On a piece of paper, draw a puzzle outline with space for seven key ideas. Then write the seven key points from the lecture you plan to give. Cut the puzzle into the seven pieces. Make enough puzzles for all students. After you have covered a key point of the lecture, stop and give each student that piece of the puzzle. Discuss it more and see if anyone has a question. Continue lecturing until you have covered another key point from the lecture. Again stop and discuss it. Continue thus until you have distributed all seven pieces of the puzzle. Then have the students put their puzzles together and review again the key ideas.
- One of my favorite activities is to play a clue type game prior to lecturing about a section in a book. I hide around the room sticky notes with clues about something we will discuss. I usually hide seven or eight clues and put the most beneficial clue in the hardest place to find. Students have to move around the room to find the various clues and see who can solve the mystery.
- Use a graphic organizer to introduce the topic and to provide an overview of what is to come. Many different types of graphic organizers are available—the teacher might use a Venn diagram for compare and contrast, or the teacher may draw a box in the middle with the key idea and then provide lines out to additional boxes that explain the key idea. Software programs that offer graphic organizers are even available.
- Prior to introducing a lecture topic, provide a group of students with a large sheet of paper and have them write down everything they

already know about the topic. You can then discuss the results with the group, and you will quickly learn which students know a great deal about the topic. You can then incorporate their knowledge into the lecture.

- At first you may want to fill in many of the points of the lecture in an outline and give students a copy of it before the lecture. You can then gradually over the course of several lectures reduce the number of points you provide the students, until you are just providing a skeletal outline. This is called a fading approach, giving the student the maximum number of cues in the beginning and then reducing the number. Some students will need a longer time before you can reduce the number of cues. The teacher can vary the outlines according to the specific needs of the students.

- Begin the lecture with an attention grabber. For example, start a lecture by playing Two Truths and a Lie. In this game, three statements about the upcoming lecture are provided. Two of the statements are true and one of them is a lie. Students have to guess which statement is the lie. The teacher requests a response from each student. Secondary students, in particular, really like this activity at the beginning of a topic.

- Let your students know ahead of time that during the next ten minutes of your lecture you will include a mistake in the information you provide and it is their job to catch the mistake. The student who catches the mistake should raise a hand and let you know the mistake you made. In the beginning, make sure you make an obvious mistake so it is easy for the students to catch it. Then you can make one that is harder to accept. If no one catches the mistake, then stop in seven to ten minutes and discuss the major points in the lecture and discuss what information is incorrect and why.

- Pace the lesson so you can keep student attention. Move quickly through easy parts of the lecture and more slowly through difficult parts.

- Provide a handout to each student with a picture of a person and a blank bubble for a question, as well as a picture of a person with a blank bubble for an answer. During the lecture, stop at a given point and have each student write a question the student has about the topic. Then assign students to a partner with whom they exchange papers. Both individuals should write down an answer to the other's question.

- Use visuals with the verbal information. You will certainly want to incorporate pictures to explain your points. Connor and Lagares (2007) discuss the use of pictures to teach about the Bill of Rights—for example, a picture of a human head with an open mouth would depict free speech. Even better is the use of objects to illustrate your point. If you are lecturing about a given country, items from the country will make the lecture more meaningful for the student. Wearing a costume from that country also will make the lecture more interesting to the students.

- Stop every five to seven minutes and have students compare notes with a partner. Pair a more capable student with a less capable student.

- Utilize signals. For example, say, "This is a key point" or "Remember this idea." You could vary your voice tone—for instance, raise it slightly when making a key point.

- Use response cards when asking questions. Instead of asking questions and having students raise their hand if they know the answers, provide index cards, small chalkboards, or whiteboards, and have the students write the answers on those cards or boards. When they are finished, they hold up their boards or cards. You also can make a statement and ask students to stand up if they agree with the statement or stay seated if the do not agree. Or you can use a thumbs-up or thumbs-down response (Johns, Crowley, & Guetzloe, 2002). Smartboards are an excellent way to provide multiple opportunities for students to observe a wealth of information and to provide active responses. The teacher quickly sees how many students have provided a correct answer and can use that knowledge as a cue to reteach the information.

- Incorporate wait time into your lecture. Wait time is defined as an "instructional delivery procedure that uses a pause (three to five seconds) between a teacher question and a student response" (Haydon, Borders, Embury, & Clarke, 2009, p. 15). The wait time allows students to process the information and formulate an answer to the question. Research over a significant period of time has shown that there will be improvements in both language and logic when the teacher uses the procedure (Haydon, Borders, Embury, & Clarke, 2009).

- Try lecture bingo. Prior to the lecture, choose key terms that you will be discussing in the lecture. Using blank bingo cards, put one term in each square until the card is filled. Each child gets a different bingo card. Students are asked to listen closely to the lecture. When you say a term that is on the student's bingo card, the student is instructed to mark the square. When a student gets a straight line or diagonal line, the student yells "bingo" (Johns & Crowley, 2007).

- Use the students' names when giving an example. This will personalize the lecture.

- Use proximity control. That is, move around the room while lecturing and stay close to students who may have difficulty. Avoid being obvious about this, though, so you do not embarrass the student.

- Summarize the key points at the end of the lecture. Highlight the key points, introduce what will be discussed next, and review follow-up assignments. The teacher should choose five or six key points that have been discussed during the lecture and then review those with the students. Or the teacher might ask students to write down the important points of the lecture and then have an active discussion of those points, indicating whether students agree with the key points. It is fun to have the students share the points with the teacher and then to see which ones were the most important according to the students. It is also fun to create suspense about what is coming up next—the teacher can give the students a teaser about the upcoming activities. For example, if the teacher will be discussing foods that were commonly eaten during the Great Depression, the teacher might lead with the statement, "Tomorrow I am going to give you a taste of some foods that you may or may not like." To review the assignments to be completed, the teacher can have the students discuss those with their neighbor.

- Have students repeat key facts in unison (Yehle & Warmbold, 1998). The advantage of doing this is that it provides students with additional auditory feedback about what the key facts are. Some children not only need to see the information, but they need to hear the information and speak it aloud. This assists students in remembering key facts.

- Incorporate movement as much as possible. For example, prepare ahead of time a set of index cards. On one set of cards, put questions; on another set, write answers. Give each student a card. Students are then to find the matching question or answer. As mentioned in the previous chapter, this is also an excellent way to break students into pairs for an assignment.

- Play Lend Me Your Ear. To keep the attention of the students, give each student a small piece of paper with a word that you will be using some time during the lecture. When you say the word in your lecture, the student who has the paper is to stand up and say, "I have _____ word" (Tilton, 2005).

- The games like Jeopardy or Who Wants to Be a Millionaire can stimulate interest in the topic being taught. Use such games to review your lecture material, and they are a good way for you to informally assess whether your students have retained the key points. Teachers can find Jeopardy or Who Wants to Be a Millionaire games online.

- Include praise throughout the lecture. It is critical that the teacher move around the room while lecturing and praise those students who are attending and giving correct responses. Teachers can foster learning even further by providing praise when a student offers an answer that is correct and specific, and then by supplying additional related or novel information to the student at the same time. The teacher then is not only giving praise for an appropriate response but is expanding the feedback by providing additional information to the students (Conroy, Sutherland, Snyder, Al-Hendawi, & Vo, 2009).

Summary: Just 3×5 It

1. Teachers can use attention grabbers to begin the lecture, such as Two Truths and a Lie.

2. It's a good idea to provide introductory activities prior to the lecture using puzzles, clues, graphic organizers, outlines, and flip chart fill ups (students fill a whole sheet with what they already know about the topic).

3. A fun technique is for the teacher to make mistakes while lecturing and see if students can find them.

4. Educators can pair visual with auditory information.

5. Incorporating wait time into the lecture is essential.

6. Teachers can incorporate active responding, using no tech (response cards) or high-tech (Smartboards) devices.

7. Activities such as lecture bingo, Lend Me Your Ear, proximity control, and use of student names, can be an effective way to keep the attention of some students during the lecture.

8. Educators can also incorporate games, movement, and reviews into lectures.

Worksheet Adaptations

"**I** ain't doing that worksheet," "I don't want to do all these math problems," "This is too hard." How many times have you heard these remarks from a student when you present yet another worksheet? We seem to use so many worksheets in our school—drill and practice; yet for some of our children we are creating worksheet wars. Some of our children don't like doing paperwork and we give them a lot of it to do and wonder why they are so frustrated. I admit I am not a worksheet lover because so many of the worksheets that are used in today's schools are overwhelming to our students with special needs or are difficult to understand.

I was saying to a colleague that I wished I could ban worksheets from today's classrooms and she quickly reminded me that we live in a paperwork society and that individuals will always be required to do paperwork, so by giving students worksheets we are preparing them to complete forms. She also reminded me that some children like to do worksheets so I had to admit to myself that there was some truth to what she said. We shouldn't completely eliminate worksheets, but we ought to rethink how we present them. We also need to rethink the quantity of worksheets that we give to students and whether the use of worksheets can be substituted by an activity that may be more meaningful to the student.

McKinney and colleagues (2009) reported on a survey conducted with mathematics teachers in urban schools and found that 64 percent of teachers use drill and practice rather than student-centered activities. Much of that drill and practice is in the form of worksheets.

This chapter talks about some of the problems with today's worksheets and how we can make them easier and more user friendly for our students. The chapter also provides some alternatives to worksheets.

THE PROBLEMS WITH TODAY'S WORKSHEETS

A few years ago, a friend of mine who is a parent of a fifth-grade child with specific learning disabilities showed me a math test that a teacher had given to her son—he had received a D on the test. She was very upset and asked me to look at the test. I was shocked at what I saw: the test had been handwritten by the teacher, it was double-sided with no comment that the student needed to turn the page over, there were at least six different sets of directions on the test and the directions were hard to understand, and no examples were supplied. It was easy to see why the child with a learning disability had difficulty with the test. He was bothered by the amount of clutter on the page—very little white space was available. He had difficulty changing directions in the middle of the page and was still following the first set of directions when he should have been following the sixth set. He also had difficulty reading the teacher's handwriting. Hopefully not many people would present such a difficult test for this child. Technology makes it easy for us to now input our tests or worksheets, enlarge the print, accent the changes in directions, and more.

As I look at worksheets I see some common problems. Often there is more than one set of directions on a single worksheet. On some worksheets, I have seen the directions change six times. This is so difficult for a student with special needs who may have difficulty attending to the change in directions and has difficulty "switching gears" on the same page. Some of our students who perseverate do so on the first set of directions and just keep going the same way as they did when they began the worksheet.

Some worksheets use one column only; students read one question, answer it, and then move on to the next question, working from top to bottom. However, on math sheets the student must move from left to right and then move down to the next row and begin again. I also see worksheets with problems in two columns, so the student moves top to bottom in one column and then has to go to the top again and work down the page in the second column. Or the student may be expected to work on the first problem in the first column and then move to the second column and then back to the first column. My point is that this is very difficult for a student who has difficulty with directionality or has difficulty keeping his or her place on a sheet of paper. Even though some worksheets may number the individual problems as a guiding tool for the students, some students are so focused on the actual problems that they pay no attention to the numbering system.

Prior to beginning any worksheet that changes the presentation format that the student is used to, it is critical that the teacher review the sequence of completion.

I once heard it said that if we could make tests with more white space, we might achieve greater results from students. Students need space—some children can't fit the answer into the small space that is allowed. The student might write big and become very frustrated trying to fit an answer in a space that is too small. The student may end up drawing arrows to where the answers are completed.

Many worksheets are just too busy. It is fine to decorate worksheets but putting a favorite character in the worksheet to stimulate interest means that you will need to reduce the amount of work on that sheet. Some students may focus on extraneous details and won't focus on the task they must complete.

Some worksheets include vocabulary with which the students are unfamiliar. Children may not understand the words in the directions or may not understand the particular words used in a comprehension question or math problem. A teacher of first graders reported to me that in many of the worksheets she used, the direction was to "draw a circle around the correct answer." One day she gave the children a worksheet with the directions: "Draw a ring around the correct answer." Many of the children looked very confused and she figured out why—they were not familiar with that word as a direction—they knew ring as something you wore on your hand or something that you used to swim.

ADAPTING THE APPEARANCE AND CONTENT OF WORKSHEETS

This section provides helpful tips for reviewing whether the worksheets given to students are user friendly for them.

- It is critical that the teacher review the worksheet in advance to determine whether any students will have difficulty understanding whether they should complete the information left to right, top to bottom, or one column and then the next. If the student may have difficulty in directionality, you may want to make small arrows that will direct the student on the appropriate order in which the information should be completed, because just numbering the problems may not be sufficient.
- Review also the vocabulary used in the worksheet's directions. It is critical that the students understand all those words in order to complete the worksheet.
- Increase the white space to provide more room for students to write their answers. In our zeal to save paper, we often don't provide the student sufficient space to write and the student becomes frustrated with the lack of space given. Think about the size of a student's writing and make sure to leave enough space to actually answer the question.

- Avoid more than one set of directions on one page. Since this is difficult for students with special needs, every effort should be made to provide a single set of directions on a page. If this is not possible, then at least highlight and review the directions with the student or draw a line to separate one section of the worksheet from the previous one.
- Block out part of the page for children who are visually distracted. You can put the worksheet in a file folder that has the front section cut into strips (see Chapter 2 for details). You also can fold the worksheet in half for the student.
- Provide only one worksheet at a time to avoid overwhelming the student. Presenting a single worksheet rather than a work packet, or giving shorter assignments at one time, is positively associated with relieving students' stress (Niesyn, 2009).
- Use worksheets as a model for teaching children how to write. Acrey, Johnstone, and Milligan (2005) stress that when teachers write in complete sentences rather than in phrases on worksheets, they are assisting students in understanding how to apply the rules of grammar. We must be very careful not to include too many abbreviations or shortcuts with our students because then we do not show them how to write in complete sentences. A number of us utilize PowerPoint and we have become what I call "bulleted point thinkers." This is okay when summarizing key points, but if we do this too much we are not teaching the student how to compose a complete sentence. Recently a colleague of mine received a term paper from a student who had used the abbreviations that we use today in text messages. While we live in a world of text messaging, those abbreviations usually are inappropriate in other writing.
- Look closely at the size and appearance of the type. We often may want to enliven the appearance of the teacher-made worksheet so we employ an unusual typeface that ends up being difficult for the student to read. The type is a critical consideration when the teacher is creating a document for the student. Times Roman, Helvetica, and Arial are common types to use, but sans serif fonts such as Helvetica and Arial are more like hand lettering and therefore readers can easily recognize letters and words. Acrey, Johnstone, and Milligan (2005) recommend 14- or 18-point type as the standard for lower grades; 12-point type can be used for older students. Enlarge the print even more for students who are overwhelmed by too much text on one page.
- Use bold type or italics for key words. Avoid using capital letters for long sentences because they are harder for a student to read—a student can't use the shape of letters to aid in word recognition. Capital letters can be used for titles. Underlining makes words harder for the student to read, so use bold type or italics instead (Acrey, Johnstone, & Milligan, 2005).

- Provide necessary cues for the student. When you have created a worksheet that is two-sided, always remember to put *(over)* at the bottom of the first page so the student knows that more questions can be found on the other side of the paper. But the teacher must be sure to check whether the students understand what *(over)* means. After giving the students the worksheet, the teacher should review the directions and then remind the students to turn the page over. Another option is to print in large type: *Turn the paper over to the other side.* If a question on the worksheet has two parts, the student may be likely to complete only the first part and forget to do the second part. Highlight the second part in the directions.

HOW TO MAKE WORKSHEETS MORE FUN AND APPEALING FOR STUDENTS

For those students who may not want to complete a worksheet, we need to make the activity a more desirable one for them. Here are some ideas that I have used to make those dreaded (in the eyes of some of our students) worksheets more fun for them.

- Have the student roll dice to see how many problems or questions to complete on the worksheet.
- Give the student choices. The student can do the odd numbered problems or the even numbered problems. The student can pick any six. The student can do the worksheet with a red pencil or a green pencil. More information on the importance of choices is found in Chapter 5.
- Try carousel brainstorming (also discussed in Chapter 7). Arrange students in a group of eight around a table or students can form their desks in a circle. All students have a copy of the worksheet. Each student completes the first two questions, then when the music starts the students pass the worksheet to the person on their left, who does the next two on the sheet. The worksheet keeps getting passed around the table until it is completed. Students finish all the problems but it does not seem as overwhelming, and the teacher can check how well each student did.
- Prepare students to do worksheets independently using "I do, we do, you do together, you do." Prior to distributing a worksheet, the teacher answers the first question or problem for the students. The students then do a problem or question together. Then they are divided into pairs or teams to do a problem or question together. And last, the student works independently to complete the remainder of the worksheet.

- Take advantage of the Nintendo effect (Wright & Gurman, 1994). The Nintendo effect (also discussed in Chapter 5) is based on the premise that we need to capitalize on the interests of the students. With the Nintendo effect, the student who has completed a math assignment gets to play with the Nintendo. However, I vary the Nintendo effect by building the high preference activity into the worksheet, essentially using the high interest activity like the Nintendo game. If the student loves trains, consider putting trains on the worksheet and putting the math problems inside the train engine or the caboose. If the student likes Superman, draw pictures of Superman on the sheet and put the math problems on Superman's chest. If the student loves to go to McDonald's, use the McDonald's menu for math and reading.

ALTERNATIVES TO WORKSHEETS

Many activities can be used as alternatives to worksheets. These activities show the teacher the student has understood the content but reduces the "paperwork" that the student must complete or presents the paperwork in a less overwhelming manner.

Traveling Assignment

I was working with a teacher in an after school program and she was very frustrated because every day the fifth grader diagnosed with ADHD with whom she was assigned to work would come in with several math worksheets and he would announce he wasn't doing all that work. I asked her if she had access to a copy machine, which she did. I suggested she take each sheet and cut it up into four or five sections. She then could take the sections and tape them up around the room. She would then give the student a clipboard and a blank sheet of paper. He could walk around the room going to one area where one of the sections was taped. There he would complete that section of the worksheet. When he was done with one section, he would then move to another section until the entire worksheet was completed. He could choose the order in which he did the sections. After the student had answered all the questions, he, with the teacher's assistance, could then copy the answers on to the whole worksheet. This proved to be invaluable to the teacher since the student could move, the worksheet was broken down into small segments, and the student could choose the order in which he did the task.

Red Rubber Ball

In Chapter 2, I discuss the use of the red rubber ball on which the teacher writes math problems or various questions. The student has to toss and catch the ball and solve the problem or answer the question under her or his left thumb. The student then writes the answer on a sheet of paper. The teacher can request that the student do ten problems or questions.

Concentration/Memory

For studying math problems or vocabulary words, or for answering questions, the teacher can put the problems or questions on one set of index cards and the answers on others. The students can play a game where they turn all the cards over and try to match each one. The teacher can work with a student to see whether the student actually can match the problems with the answers. This is certainly appropriate for all ages of students and makes the process of learning information more fun.

The Gum Ball Machine

At a dollar store, you can purchase a gum ball machine. You can put different color gum balls in it and students get one of the balls out of the machine. The teacher can then code the worksheets for a particular type of activity: the student who gets a red ball has to do a certain sheet or assignment; a green one indicates a different sheet, and so on. Another option is the student who gets a red ball has to draw a picture about the topic; if it's a blue ball then make a game; if it's a yellow ball then write a song. The possibilities are many and this makes the process so much more fun. This also is appropriate with varying ages of students.

Bingo Cards

The teacher can fill in the squares of a blank bingo card with math problems or social studies questions. Students then get to choose any five to complete in order to make a bingo. Or the teacher can require them to make a letter X on the card, so that the students complete ten problems. The bingo games can be varied to keep up the interest of the students.

Fill in the different squares writing prompts, and have students write the story using any five of the prompt words that would make a bingo.

For spelling, students can begin by choosing any five words to study. Once those are mastered, they move on to the next five, and so on until the bingo card is completed.

Teacher-made bingo cards can be laminated so that you can reuse them multiple times. Small laminators are coming down in cost all the time. When one of my students who is getting ready to become a teacher was asked by her mother what she wanted for the holidays, she replied that she wanted a small laminator.

Tablecloth or Shower Curtain Answers

The teacher can write a series of numbers with a permanent marker on a plastic tablecloth or a shower curtain that can then be laid out on the floor. The student working on a math problem can move to the correct answer on the sheet. This is a good activity for younger students. For students from the second to fifth grades, it can be a team game in which the team members take turns moving to the appropriate square.

Roll the Dice

The teacher can either use a set of number dice or can purchase blank dice and write on them. In the case of number dice, the students get to roll them to determine how many problems or questions to answer on the worksheet. In the case of blank dice, the teacher can write different assignments on a die, then the student can roll it to determine what assignment to do.

Tic-Tac-Toe

This activity is appropriate for students from fourth grade on (Johns & Crowley, 2007). Students younger would probably have some difficulty making three choices out of a possible nine options. Instead of a worksheet, the teacher can give each student a tic-tac-toe sheet with nine possible assignments. The students choose any three assignments to make a tic-tac-toe. I have also used this as an assessment tool. The squares may include such assignments as write a letter to the editor about this topic, write ten true and false questions with the answers, write a poem about the topic, make a game about the topic, and write a skit about the topic. The possibilities are endless and students get a choice of assignments.

Pick Your Post

In pick your post, the teacher provides instruction on a given topic. Students then have a follow-up assignment to complete. The teacher can post around the room five or six different assignments to supplement the instruction. The assignments might include make a game about this topic, write a skit about the topic, make a graphic organizer about what you have learned, create a video production of what you have learned, make a PowerPoint about the topic, and so on. The students then go to the particular post that depicts the assignment that they wish to complete. The teacher can set it up so that the students work individually on the post or can consider having the students work as a group to complete the assignment, or the teacher can give the students a choice of whether they want to work independently or in a group.

Summary: Just 3×5 It

1. Multiple challenges exist in today's worksheets: multiple directions on one page, lack of adequate space, unfamiliar vocabulary, and too much information on one page.

2. Teachers should avoid distributing too many worksheets at one time.

3. Teachers should review worksheets in advance to determine problem areas such as vocabulary words and size of type.

4. Teachers should provide necessary cues for students to complete the worksheets.

5. Teachers can prepare students in advance to do worksheets through such activities as I do, we do, you do together, you do.

6. Teachers should make efforts to ensure that worksheets are fun and appealing to students.

7. Traveling assignments provide opportunities for movement for students.

8. Teachers can incorporate choices into worksheets through tic-tac-toe, pick your post, and bingo.

5

Behavioral Adaptations

"I think he can learn, but his behavior sure gets in the way." "She just won't follow directions. She is so busy telling all of her friends what to do that she doesn't do what she is supposed to do." "Sometimes I feel like I have used everything in my bag of tricks to get him to work and he just won't do anything." An increasing number of students are coming into classrooms with these behavioral challenges voiced by their teachers. Such students can be very frustrating to the teacher, as well as being disruptive to their peers and the classroom environment.

What comes first—does the behavior cause academic problems or do academic problems cause behavioral problems? While research suggests that a relationship exists between academics and behavior, we can't always answer the question which came first. Academic variables can function as aversive stimuli for many students with behavioral challenges (Hagan-Burke, Burke, & Sugai, 2007). If students perceive that the work is too difficult or they don't see a reason to learn the material being taught, the student can resort to behavioral problems. The student who fears failing at a task may resort to avoidance techniques or attention-getting devices to escape the task. Our job as educators is to increase the academic success of children so that behavioral problems are likely to decrease. If students are engaged in successful activities within the classroom and are recognized for their efforts, their behavior may improve.

The adaptations for behavioral problems in this chapter are effective for very young children as well as young adults. The first section of the chapter provides preventive strategies. The bulk of the chapter includes positive behavioral strategies, fun ways to provide positive recognition for appropriate behavior, interest-based interventions, and strength-based interventions. The chapter concludes with information about self-management strategies—those strategies that allow students to manage their own behavior so that they no longer need the external controls, achieving inner control as a lifelong skill.

PREVENTIVE BEHAVIORAL TECHNIQUES

There are many behavioral problems that can be reduced or completely eliminated if we use preventive techniques designed to keep the behavioral problem occurring in the first place. We have all heard the old adage: an ounce of prevention is worth a pound of cure. Good teachers set the stage in their classrooms to prevent behavior problems. Critical planning is a key. This section of the chapter provides an array of preventive techniques that set the stage for student success and a reduction in behavioral problems.

Preventing Behavioral Problems
With the Three Ps of Expectations/Rules

When students enter into new situations, they need to know what the "laws of the land" are. If they don't know what is expected of them, it is more likely that they will unknowingly violate a rule. Different teachers have different sets of rules, and teachers have different rules for different situations. What the teacher expects of the students during a structured lesson is probably different than what the teacher expects when students are out at recess or when they go on a field trip.

When it comes to rules, keep in mind the three Ps: Rules should be *posted* so the students have a visual reminder of what they are. They should be *positively stated*. And rules should be accompanied by *pictures* for clarification.

Rules that are posted are a frequent reminder to students of what is expected of them in the particular setting. At the beginning of the day, the teacher can verbally remind students of the rules, using the visual reminder. When a student misbehaves, rather than correcting the student, the teacher might simply say, "What do you need to do to follow rule #3." Hall rules, cafeteria rules, bus rules, and playground rules all should be posted for students to see each day.

For every negative behavior, there is a positive behavior, and the educator wants to build on positive behaviors. So rules should be stated positively. Rules such as raise your hand before speaking, ask permission to use the pencil sharpener, or keep your hands and feet to yourself are all worded positively. Many schools and classrooms have three rules, such as "Respect self, respect others, and respect property." They teach the students what respecting others actually means—keeping hands and feet to one's self, listening when others are talking, and so on. Not only should rules be stated positively, but students should receive positive recognition when they follow the rules, such as "Thanks for remembering to raise your hand."

Pictures of students following the rules should accompany the narrative. You may assume that this only applies to young students who can't read the rules, therefore it is necessary to have pictures about the rules. However, the use of pictures is applicable for older students as well.

Children with special needs require clear delineation of what is expected of them; they need structure and routine. While this topic is also discussed in Chapter 10 on time adaptations, it is also important to discuss picture schedules here in the context of behavioral adaptations. We know the importance of visual cues for students. They need a posted schedule and they need posted rules that they can see and that can be reviewed with them aloud. As students grow older we think that picture cues are no longer necessary, because the students can read and understand what is meant. However, additional visual cues are important. For example, if the rule in a classroom is to raise your hand before you speak, the teacher can include a picture of a student raising a hand beside the written rule. This way the students see what the expected behavior looks like. If the rule is to keep your hands and feet to yourself, a picture of a student who is paying attention and in the appropriate pose would depict this. Alongside a rule about respect for property might be a picture of a student throwing away a piece of trash.

Teachers can incorporate a number of fun activities into the classroom to make the rules more memorable and meaningful for students. Rule quizzes might be employed. The teacher can plan a skit about the rules—for example, with teenagers, I use to have fun having skits about the dress code rules. The teacher can show a short video clip from which students have to pick out what classroom rules were violated.

A mnemonic I also use for the creation of rules is SPORT. That is, rules should be:

S—Short. The number of words in each rule should be few. For example: Raise your hand before speaking, or respect property.

P—Positive. Rules should be stated in a positive manner. Rather than saying don't do this and don't do that, the positive behavior should be stated in the rule (see the fair pair section later in this chapter). For example: Keep your hands and feet to yourself.

O—Observable. Rules should be such that they could be depicted in a picture so the student can see what the rule looks like. If the rule is observable, it is much easier to determine whether the student is following the rule and easier to reinforce the student for following the rule.

R—Reinforceable. Use recognition with positive reinforcement with those students who follow the rules. This chapter stresses the importance of positive recognition for students who do what they are supposed to do. When students follow rules, we should not take it for granted; we should thank them for doing so. That way we increase the possibility that the student will continue to follow the rule.

T—Teachable. It is critical that we explain to the student the meaning of the rule. For instance, in a school with a rule to respect others, the educator must teach the student what respecting others means, such as keeping hands and feet to one's self or listening while others are talking.

Prevention Through Precorrection

One of the best adaptations for behavior problems is to prevent such behaviors from occurring in the first place. Teachers know their students and know when a particularly difficult situation is coming up for a student. The teacher can prevent trouble through precorrection, a proactive approach. The difference between precorrection and correction is that precorrection occurs before the expected behavior, whereas correction occurs after the expected inappropriate behavior. The advantage of precorrection is that it reduces the amount of time that a teacher has to spend dealing with disruptions. If students are allowed to get off task or engage in inappropriate behavior, it takes more of the teacher's time to get the students back on task than it would to remind them of the appropriate behavior in the first place (Lampi, Fenty, & Beaunae, 2005). As an example, if the teacher knows that the students have difficulty getting in line to go to recess or getting ready to go home, the teacher can remind the students of what is expected of them in those circumstances. Then when the students do what they are supposed to do, the teacher can reinforce the appropriate behavior. As part of precorrection, behavior rehearsal may be necessary. The teacher can show the students the appropriate behavior and then have them practice it, followed by reinforcement for the appropriate behavior.

Precorrective statements include descriptions of behavior expectations for different settings and those descriptions should be positive and specific. They should be shared with students at the very beginning of an activity, when a change in expectations arises during activities, or when transitioning to a new activity (Stormont & Reinke, 2009).

I was asked to observe, Jeffrey, a four-year-old in a preschool who had been diagnosed with ADHD. The child had been removed from the classroom by an aide, and when they returned, the rest of the class was engaged in a group activity. Jeffrey proceeded to literally jump into the group, clearly disrupting the activity. The teacher could have worked with the aide to prepare Jeffrey on how to enter the group appropriately.

Precorrection would have been very appropriate and would have set Jeffrey up for success.

Older students often don't know the expectations when they go from class to class or switch activities. Teachers should provide the clear expectations about what needs to be done before the class or activity begins.

Prevention Through Proximity

Proximity control is a very effective behavioral intervention and can prevent many behavioral problems from occurring. If the teacher wanders around the room when students are working independently or taking a quiz, she or he can see if any student is having a problem with the activity and can lend support to the student or answer a particular question. The teacher also can see exactly what is going on and remove the temptation for the students to talk out in class or to cheat on a test.

Proximity means being close, but not too close, to the student. If a student is in a crisis, the teacher should keep some distance from the student, respecting the students' space. A rule of thumb is to stay one and a half to three feet away from a student who is in crisis so that the student does not feel overwhelmed (Johns & Carr, 2009). The teacher should never get into a student's face or back the aggressive student into a corner.

Prevention Through Antiseptic Bouncing

A very effective adaptation for students who become antsy and restless during class is to look for the warning signs that trouble is brewing and to use antiseptic bouncing. When you see that a student is becoming anxious or hyper, you might suggest a trip to the pencil sharpener. You also might request that the student to take a note to the office for you. The note may just say, "Thank Sara for bringing this note to the office and tell her to have a great day and send her back to class." That short break may be all that is needed to get the student back on track. It is a wonderful preventive tool.

Prevention Through Behavior Momentum

Behavior momentum is a very effective intervention that builds on the strengths of the child in order to make the presentation of a more difficult task easier for the student to cope with. Behavior momentum is the use of a series of preferred behaviors to increase the probability that nonpreferred behaviors will occur (Lee, Belfiore, & Budin, 2008). A series of brief tasks that are likely to result in compliance are presented just prior to tasks with a low probability of compliance. The student gains momentum for success and completes the difficult task. Behavior momentum is the most effective when educators deliver praise after the compliance with the high probability or preferred tasks (Lee, 2005).

How does it work? When the teacher knows that he or she will give an assignment that the student will perceive as difficult, the teacher precedes it with two or three easy tasks that will result in success for the student. If the teacher has planned a math test for the class and Marlon, a fifth grader, reports that "I hate math," the teacher has an idea that the student will not be thrilled with the test. Marlon however loves to read and likes to show everyone in the class that he loves to read. He also likes to help the teacher. She then asks everyone in the class to clear their desks so that the test papers can be distributed by Marlon. She praises the class for clearing their desk. The teacher then asks Marlon and two other students to pass out the papers for her. When he does that, the teacher says, "Thanks, I appreciate that." The teacher then asks Marlon to read the directions to the class. After he does so, she thanks him. He has now been reinforced for three tasks that were easy for him to do and is in a more positive mind-set to take the test. The next time she may be able to reduce the number of easy tasks prior to the difficult one from three to two, and eventually reduce it to one easy task prior to a difficult task. For the success of behavior momentum, it is critical to reinforce the student for completing the easy tasks in order to set the stage for the difficult task. It is also important to reinforce the student for beginning and working on the more difficult task.

Jump Start

It's all in how you say something to a student. Anytime you word a request in a positive manner, it is more likely that the student will comply with your request. One example is letting a student know that he or she has work to be done. If the teacher says to the student, "You have lots to get done so you better get it all done," the student becomes overwhelmed before even getting started. However, if the teacher says, "I need you to start your math," the student is more likely to begin. If you think about it, when you get behind in your work, you become overwhelmed; however, if you just decide to start on a project and work on it for five to ten minutes, you are more likely to keep going and get more done. Feeling overwhelmed only leads to avoidance behaviors.

Fair Pair

A long history of research shows us that if we want to encourage a behavior, we need to reinforce the positive behavior that we want. This is not bribing; it is recognizing the student for a job well done. Oftentimes when students have behavior problems, we draw attention to their negative behavior and forget to recognize their appropriate behavior. What then happens? The student continues to act up because she or he receives attention for inappropriate behavior, rather than receiving attention for the opposite, appropriate behavior. When a student's negative behavior frustrates us, we need to consider the "fair pair"—the opposite, appropriate behavior that we want to increase. For example, I often hear that the student is engaging in work refusal: "He just won't do anything." Therefore when the student is in the classroom and refusing to work, the teacher may correct, plead, and even beg the student to do the work. What does the student do? Continue to refuse to do the work. The fair pair is engagement in the assigned task. The teacher praises the student when the student is working. "Thanks for starting on your math" or "I sure like the way you are working away at that English." Having worked with many passive aggressive students during my career, I learned quickly that begging and pleading cause a student to dig in his or her heels even more. The technique doesn't work. It is critical that the teacher not become upset with the student because the student may be very reinforced by that. The teacher instead must recognize the student for the appropriate behavior. If students are running in the hall, instead of yelling at the students for that behavior, the teacher needs to recognize the students who are walking in the hall and say, "Thanks for walking in the hall."

The fair pair also is known as the replacement behavior, the one that you desire to replace an inappropriate behavior. The replacement behavior for work refusal is active engagement in the task or work completion. For any negative behavior that bothers you, you must consider the specific appropriate behavior that you want. This is the opposite, appropriate behavior—the replacement behavior.

Attributions

"Attribution is the way that an individual explains to himself the cause of his success or failure" (Johns, McGrath, & Mathur, 2010, p. 51). It is important that we teach our students to attribute their success to their own efforts. Oftentimes students don't believe that they are responsible for their achievement. They tend to attribute their accomplishments to an outside force such as luck, the fact that the task was easy, or something the teacher did (Lerner & Johns, 2009). It is critical that we teach our students from an early age that their success is due to their own efforts. Statements such as "You got an A on that test because you studied hard" or "You got all that work done because you stuck with it" show students that they have controlled their own success. Good teachers work with their students to teach them to associate successes with controllable factors such as effort, persistence, and the correct use of learning or cognitive strategies. They teach students what they actually did to succeed (Margolis & McCabe, 2003).

Behavior-Specific Praise

Once the educator has identified the fair pair or the opposite, appropriate behavior, the teacher must then reinforce that behavior and reinforce it frequently until the behavior becomes a habit for the student. If the student has been engaging in work refusal, then when the student picks up the pen and starts working, the teacher needs to praise the student for the specific, desired behavior: "Thank you for starting your assignment." Praise by the teacher is more effective when it is behavior specific. Such praise indicates to the student the specific behavior that elicits the praise—it communicates to the student the expectation that the teacher has. Behavior-specific praise eliminates problem behaviors and works with even the most challenging students. It also reduces the need for reprimands and increases your positive interactions with your students (Brophy, 1983; Reinke, Lewis-Palmer, & Merrell, 2008; Stormont & Reinke, 2009).

Many teachers report using positive reinforcement, but when data is gathered on the actuality of praise statements within the classroom, it appears they don't really use that much praise. The teacher may praise certain students a lot more than other students. The teacher might praise students more at the beginning of the day than at the end of the day. Teachers must consistently strive to increase their use of positive reinforcement, especially for some students who may have behavioral problems. The students with behavioral problems may be getting hardly any, if any, reinforcement, and therefore end up causing more behavior problems. The teacher can increase the use of reinforcement in a number of ways.

- **Audiotaping a certain period of the day.** If a teacher notices more behavioral problems at certain times of the day, the teacher can choose that thirty or forty minute period and audiotape record himself or herself for purposes of self-monitoring. At the end of the day the teacher listens to the tape, making note of the number of general praise statements, the number of behavior-specific praise statements, and the number of reprimands that were made. The teacher then set improvement goals. It is important to be clear that the teacher is recording herself or himself and not the students. The teacher uses this tape solely for self-improvement, not to gather information about the student. If the teacher wishes to use this tape to monitor student behavior, then parent permission would be required and the tape would become part of the student record.
- **Pennies in your pocket.** The teacher can put a supply of pennies in one pocket at the beginning of the day. For each positive statement the teacher makes to a student, one penny gets moved from the starting pocket to another pocket. The goal for the teacher is to move all of the pennies to the other pocket by the end of the day.
- **Bingo for reinforcement.** Bingo can be used to assist the teacher in monitoring his or her own use of positive reinforcement. Bingo cards can be created that have twenty-five praise statements that might be made in a school day: thanks for raising your hand, I like the way you waited your turn, thanks for lining up quietly. The

teacher then gives each student one of these bingo cards. Each time the teacher speaks one of the praise statements, students can mark that square on their cards. The first student to have a bingo gets some type of recognition. This assists the teacher in monitoring the use of reinforcement and recognizes the students for appropriate behavior.

- **Personal positive notes.** Some students, particularly older students, may not like to be praised in front of their peers. In those cases, an alternative to verbal reinforcement is to write a short positive note, perhaps on a sticky note, to the student, approach the student, and put the note on the student's desk. The note can just say, "Wow— great answer to the question" or "Thanks for paying attention." Some teachers keep a supply of blank sheets of paper for this purpose on their desk every day and work to make sure that all the paper is used for positive notes. Personal notes can and should be sent to families as well. The parent may have remembered to send the signed field trip permission in or may have worked on the homework assigned with their child. The teacher sends a short thank-you note home to the parent, and the parent is hearing from the school for a positive reason. I have seen some teachers who have postcards printed that say something like "Great news from Mrs. Johns's class." Then the teacher can address the card and write a short positive note on it. Again, if you are going to do this, set a goal to do so many each day or each week.

FUN WAYS TO REINFORCE APPROPRIATE BEHAVIOR

Some teachers operate very elaborate point and level systems within classrooms. This book does not deal with the intricacies of how to set up a point system. For more information on the pros and cons of such systems, you will want to refer to other books that are devoted to the topic (Johns, Crowley, & Guetzloe, 2002). This book offers some easy and fun ways to reinforce appropriate behavior that are relatively easy to implement. They also make the school day more fun and exciting for both you and the children. The excitement and enthusiasm that these ideas generate are well worth the time and effort.

Tickets

You can purchase raffle tickets. When you observe a student behaving appropriately, give that student one half of a raffle ticket and put the other half in a basket. You can then have a raffle at the end of the day for a special prize or treat.

Coupons

A number of schools give students special coupons that can be either collected to earn a prize or turned in at the end of the day for a drawing.

Bingo Cards

There are a number of options for reinforcing student behavior by using bingo cards. I have used them for improving the school attendance of students with serious truancy problems. For example, a student is given a blank bingo card. Each day he comes to school he gets to color in a bingo square. When he gets five, he earns a choice of a prize. Some schools are laminating large bingo cards and putting them up on the wall in elementary cafeterias. When a class follows the rules for the day, they get to color in a square. When they get a bingo, the class gets a special treat or an extra five minutes at lunch. Teachers also can give students a bingo card with blank squares. When the student is behaving, the teacher can request that the student color in a square of the bingo card.

Catch-Them-Being-Good Notes

When the teacher sees a student engaging in a positive behavior, the teacher gives the student a special notes. The teacher can set a number of notes that students need to collect in order to get some special privilege, or the notes themselves may be motivating enough for some students.

Marbles in the Jar

Periodically, when the teacher sees the student or class behaving appropriately, he or she puts a marble in the jar. The goal is to fill up the marble jar. When the marble jar is full, the students receive some special treat—it could be a fun and preferred activity.

Gum Ball Machine

Fill a small gum ball machine (which can be purchased at a dollar store). A student who has had a period of appropriate behavior is allowed to get a gum ball out of the machine.

Reinforcers in a Jar

The teacher can write different reinforcers on small sheets of paper, such as take a five minute break, pick out a special pencil with a particular smell, pick out an eraser, you have earned five minutes of extra computer time, and so on. When the student has done well for a period of time, she or he may draw a reinforcer out of the jar.

A Spin of the Wheel

The teacher can get a wheel that spins and place reinforcers on each of the sections of the wheel. A good day earns the student a spin the wheel at the end of the day.

Mystery Motivator

The mystery motivator delivers an unknown but appealing reward for engaging in appropriate behavior (Jenson, Rhode, & Reavis, 1994). The student can earn some type of recognition for appropriate behavior but doesn't know what the recognition will be (thus the mystery motivator).

This fun activity may be implemented in a variety of ways. I used mystery motivator as a whole school activity with students with special needs from ages of six through twenty, but it easily can be used for an individual student. If I suspected that it could be a difficult day for students—weather change, school picture day, major change in schedule—I put up signs around the building and at the door where the students came into the school. The signs would have question marks on them and a statement: "This is a mystery motivator day!" Students would come in excited (yes, even the older students) and ask, "What's the mystery motivator?" I would answer, "It's a surprise—but you will find out at the end of the day if you follow the rules today." The teachers would then monitor the students, and those who had a good day would receive the mystery motivator. Our students liked the fancy pencils with the fun erasers on them, tickets for a drawing of a special prize, and food treats. I had the luxury of being able to determine when the buses left, so if the school had a higher percentage of students who earned the mystery motivator than the last time the motivator was done, I would call for the buses early and send students home five or ten minutes early. Older students really loved this.

One of the keys to success with the mystery motivator is to vary when it happens—don't do it the same day of the week—that way there is an element of surprise to when it might be.

JOURNALING AS A BEHAVIORAL ADAPTATION

For children who have difficulty calming down after something has upset them, journaling may be a good way to reduce their stress. You may work with children who, when you try to talk with them about something that has happened, become loud and upset again. Consider having them write down information about what upset them. This is not appropriate for students with written expression problems for whom written journaling would be too frustrating. However, some students can calm themselves if they are provided the opportunity to write about the problem situation.

I remember working with a teenager who often came in upset in the morning, feeling he had been wronged by the bus driver. I had him write about the event of the morning and then turn it in to me. This was a much preferred method to get him to calm down because talking to him about it would only upset him again. Younger students who cannot write might keep a picture journal of things that have happened to them.

Many teachers have students write in their journals at a certain time of the day, but some students may need to be able to write in the journal when they become upset during the day.

SIGNALS

As discussed in Chapter 2, a seventh-grade math teacher worked with a group of forty students during one of her math periods. One student had Asperger syndrome. When he became agitated or overexcited, she knew it was not a good idea to call attention to his behavior in front of the other students. She discussed the problem with me, and we came up with a signal. The teacher then met with him and they talked about a visual signal that she could provide to him when needed—a secret signal between the two of them. After she lectured the class, she would walk around the classroom with a pen in her hand. When he was becoming excited and needed to settle down, she would put a small sticky note on her pen. That was the signal for him to quiet down.

She also developed another signal for the student to use when he had a question during a lecture. He didn't want to ask a question in front of his peers, so he would pull on his ear. When she saw the signal she knew that meant he didn't understand what she had said. And if the student with Asperger syndrome didn't understand what she had said, there were probably other students who also didn't understand as well. She knew to reteach the concept.

INTEREST-BASED INTERVENTIONS

How many times have we heard a student ask, "Why do I have to learn this?" This is always a good question that should cause us to pause to see whether we can justify why we are teaching the particular topic. It is also time to pause to reflect on whether the lesson we are teaching is of interest to students so they are excited about learning. In keyboarding, we might have a student write a meaningless passage, leaving the student to wonder why she or he has to do something so boring. The student then loses interest in keyboarding. Rather than engaging in this activity, the teacher could have students write a letter to someone they know—perhaps they have a friend or relative serving in the military. Writing such a letter would give a student more reason to learn keyboarding.

Students with autism often have very specific interests, such as Superman, Power Rangers, Thomas the Tank Engine, or the weather. Years ago we spent a great deal of time working with them to reduce the number of times that they talked about those things. I can remember thinking to myself: "I don't want to hear one more thing about Superman." Now we have learned that instead of expending our energy trying to get the student to quit talking about their fixated interests, we should capitalize on them. We can use their interests in order to teach them; we can embed these interests in our activities to motivate the students.

Learning About Students' Interests and Strengths

With some students, you can determine pretty quickly where their interests lie. You also can observe what they like to do in their spare time. You may want to interview a parent to discover what the student likes to do at home. A short student interest or preference survey like the sample that follows also can be helpful.

What is your favorite TV show?

Who is your favorite singer?

If you have ten extra minutes, what do you like to do?

If you could go anywhere in the world, where would you go?

What would you like to learn more about?

What is your favorite subject?

What is your favorite food?

Where is your favorite restaurant?

What is your favorite game?

The questions can be varied, depending on the age and level of the students, but this can give you some idea about what will interest students.

The Nintendo Effect

As introduced in Chapter 4, many students like to play with their Nintendo, and the term *Nintendo effect* refers to capitalizing on a student's interest when planning academic activities (Wright & Gurman, 1994). Here are sixteen examples of ways to incorporate the Nintendo effect into a student's activities.

1. If the student loves to talk about the weather, provide time for the student to read about the weather and incorporate weather into math, science, and social studies.

2. If the student loves trains, put each math problem inside a picture of a train on a worksheet.

3. For the student who loves Superman, recognize appropriate behavior by giving a card with a picture of Superman on it. When enough cards have been collected, the student earns some type of treat.

4. I remember struggling with motivating an adolescent student to read. When I interviewed the mother about what the student liked to do, she reported that he loved to watch television. So we taught the student to read using *TV Guide.*

5. Another student I worked with loved basketball cards. When he was behaving appropriately, I first awarded him the letter *B*, then the letter *A*, then the letter *S*, and so forth. When he had spelled the phrase *basketball card*, he actually got a basketball card.

6. If the student is struggling with writing, provide a story starter with the student's favorite character.

7. Use celebrities that are of interest to the student to teach a lesson. A teacher recently told me she was preparing a lesson on stopping bullying and being positive to people. She incorporated a tape of the British singer, Susan Boyle, that showed how people were not very nice to her before they heard her begin to sing.

8. Draw a picture of a student's favorite object or character on a worksheet to brighten up the paper. When doing this, however, be very cautious that it does not make the sheet too busy or visually distracting for the student, because it then may cause the student not to work instead.

9. If the student likes crossword puzzles, instead of having the student write spelling words, have the student develop a crossword puzzle with those words.

10. Instead of drill work in math, have the student practice adding the cost of menu items from a favorite restaurant.

11. Teach reading and math by making recipes. This is also a wonderful activity on the importance of following directions.

12. Have students take a series of photos and write a story about them.

13. Have students write a story about themselves or their hobbies.

14. Have students plan a trip that they are interested in taking by drawing a map, figuring out the cost of the trip, figuring the mileage and cost of gas, and doing research on stops that could be made along the way.

15. Use students' vocational interests to teach reading, writing, and math skills.

16. In the area of working with children with autism, it has been found that, because of their fixated interests on characters such as Superman or Power Rangers, it can be effective to ask, "What would Superman do in a particular situation?"

Names in Assignments

I knew a master teacher who worked with primary age students prior to the time that computers were readily accessible. She would collect old story books and cut them up and rewrite them using the names of her students rather than the original names in the storybook. The children, many of whom had been reluctant readers, were very motivated to read the story with their names in them.

For older students, you can provide math problems that use the names of the students instead of the names of someone unknown to them. I like to write questions on tests that include names of the students. If the teacher has created problem-solving situations, students can be named in those situations.

The Premack Principle, or Grandma's Law

Remember Grandma's saying: "Eat your peas and then you get your dessert." Grandma's law is known as the Premack principle—first you need to do this and then you get to do that. It is named after David Premack (1959, 1965). The student first must do the nonpreferred or non-desired activity before getting to do the preferred, high-interest activity.

Suppose a child loves to work on the computer but does not like to participate in a group activity in the classroom. If the student works in the group activity for five minutes, then the student can work on the computer, which is the desired activity, for one or two minutes. If the student doesn't like to participate in teacher-directed activities then the teacher can establish a system in which the student works on the teacher-directed activity first and then gets to choose a preferred activity for a few minutes.

STRATEGIES TO BUILD IN STUDENT SUSPENSE AND INTEREST

I love to play games that keep students in suspense and excite them about learning. Giving students teasers about what you will do the next day motivates them to come to class. "Tomorrow we are going to play the clue game" or "I have a game of bowling planned for tomorrow" make students wonder what the next day will hold. It is important to give students something to look forward to. The following are some activities to consider (some of them are also discussed in Chapter 3 on lecture adaptations).

Two Truths and a Lie

This is one of my favorite activities at the beginning of the class period. It can actually be used to take roll with older students by having each student reply with the statement that is a lie when her or his name is called. The teacher puts three statements on the projector—two of the statements are true and one is a lie. They have to answer which statement is the lie and justify their answer.

Find the Mistake

Students love to catch their teachers in mistakes, so each morning the teacher can put one or more statements around the room. It can be a sentence with incorrect punctuation, a math problem done incorrectly, or a word spelled wrong. The students have to come in and figure out anything they can find that is wrong.

It's a Surprise

Some teachers prepare folders for their students with the worksheets that they are to complete prior to the end of the day, or the teacher will prepare a folder for homework. One of the fun things to do if you are giving folder work to students is to intersperse sheets that have a fun activity on them. The students have to complete the ones prior to the surprise in order to get to do the surprise sheet.

Clues

There are two variations of the clue game to consider. When I use clues, I like the students to get up and move, so I hide several clues around the room and the students hunt for the clues and then figure out what the answer is based on those clues. Also, students can be divided into small groups, each one with an envelope that has several clues on cards in it. Students then have to figure out the answer—it may be a particular word, a historical event, or the answer to a problem.

Who Am I?

This works well if famous people are used for the activity. The teacher gives one clue and the students have the opportunity to guess who the celebrity is. If they can't do so, they get another clue, and so forth. The earlier they guess who the person is the more points they receive.

Bowling

This is a fun way to review key information after a lesson. The teacher uses a plastic bowling set and writes key questions on each bowling pin. Students can play in teams. A student on the team throws the ball and tries to knock down as many bowling pins as possible. To get the points for knocking down the bowling pins, the team must answer the questions on each bowling pin that has been knocked down. Otherwise the team does not get the points, only those for the right answers.

Golf

For sequencing, many of us use human timelines or request that students place the cards in the right order. I also like to use the game of golf for sequencing events in order. Having acquired plastic golf clubs and plastic balls, we cleared a space in the room and put down a piece of carpet. I then list events on the inside of cones and students have to knock down the cones with their golf club and ball in the right order.

STRENGTH-BASED INTERVENTIONS

Children in today's classrooms have many different strengths. Some do well at math, some are excellent readers, some are very creative in their ability to make projects, and some love to write and do well at it. While our students with special needs struggle with some areas in learning, they excel in other areas and it is our job as educators to build on those strengths. We must give our students multiple opportunities to utilize their strengths while also working on the areas in which they struggle. Those opportunities can be built into the school day in many ways. Children need to be able to spend time during the school day excelling at what they do well. The Individuals with Disabilities Education Act of 2004 requires discussion of the strengths of the students during the Individualized Education Program (IEP) process.

We can learn more about the strengths of the students by observations, reading the IEP, reviewing other records, interviewing the students, and interviewing the parents.

This reminds me of a day when I was asked to observe in a blended preschool program where both general education students and special education students were present. I was observing a four-year-old who had been diagnosed with ADHD and exhibited some behavioral problems that had become very disruptive in the classroom. As happens with some students with behavioral problems, the teacher was really focusing on the child's negative behaviors. The students were engaged in a short playtime. One of the children had broken a mechanical toy and was very upset. The boy I was observing went over and tried to console the other child. In the meantime, the teacher came over and tried to fix the toy. The teacher was unsuccessful—she just couldn't figure it out. The boy I was observing looked at her and said, "Would you like me to fix the toy?" The teacher handed him the toy (no doubt thinking that the child could not fix it since she couldn't). The boy worked on it, and sure enough he fixed the toy.

I was observing a child because he had behavioral problems but I saw a child who was compassionate, sensitive to the needs of others, and had excellent mechanical skills for a four-year-old. Capitalizing on his strengths, I suggested that the teacher give him opportunities to help other students and also give him opportunities throughout the day to work on putting items together with his hands. He could be more successful because we would be capitalizing on his strengths.

I also can remember working with a student with Asperger syndrome who loved to talk about the weather. Instead of discouraging his talk about the weather, we capitalized on it to get him to do his work. We created math problems that were based on the weather and increased his reading by allowing him to read about the weather. In social studies, when we were studying a particular geographic area, we made sure he got to study the climate of the area.

Here are some more ways to capitalize on student strengths.

- Allow the student to help another student who does not have the same strengths.
- Use the "can do" to prevent the "can't do." If the student loves to cook and can cook well, use those cooking skills to teach the child what he or she can't do (e.g., read). Have the student read recipes to cook. If the student can take things apart and put them back together but can't read, have the student read some assembly directions. If the student is a good baseball player but can't do math, use baseball to teach math.
- Start the day with an activity that capitalizes on the student's strengths. That way the student gets off to a good start.
- Build in choice for activities and make sure that one of the choices in activities is based on the student's strength.
- If the student has good verbal skills but poor written skills, let the student voice record ideas or assignments.
- Reinforce the student for success in her or his strengths.
- Use stories about very successful individuals who had disabilities and accomplished a great deal: Tom Cruise, Albert Einstein, or Charles Schwab. This gives hope to students that they can achieve greatness based on their strengths.

CULTURALLY RESPONSIVE INTERVENTIONS

Interventions that are culturally responsive are those that build on the strengths that students bring from their home cultures instead of ignoring those strengths or utilizing interventions that are in direct conflict with their cultural values (Au, 2001; Ko, 2007). Today's classrooms reflect many different cultures and family compositions. Our students represent "a mosaic of ethnicities and cultures" (Cartledge & Kourea, 2008, p. 351). Understanding the cultural background of the student provides us with a better understanding of why the student may behave in a certain way and how the student may learn best—that is, what are the motivating factors in learning.

Culturally responsive interventions begin with the teacher's understanding of the student and family's culture. Teachers should explore the diverse cultures within their classroom, and then learn the basic tenets of those cultures. They also must show an active interest in the culture of the student and family.

Activities in this chapter about student responses, such as the use of response cards that are either low tech or high tech, are very important for these children since previous research (Greenwood, Hart, Walker, & Risley, 1994) showed that culturally and linguistically diverse students are provided few opportunities for active academic student responding.

Disciplinary actions for culturally and linguistically diverse students have long been a concern. Some of these students are disproportionately suspended or expelled from school for behaviors that may be acceptable within their culture but are not acceptable within the school setting (Cartledge & Kourea, 2008).

The following are some basic ideas for teachers to consider when planning culturally responsive interventions.

- Work to identify your own prejudices and monitor your own behavior to ensure that you are not letting those prejudices interfere with establishing a positive relationship with the student and his or her family (Turner-Vorbeck, 2005). Continually ask yourself whether you are being fair to the student or are letting your own prejudices interfere with your relationship with the child. Use self-monitoring and continual reflection of your own behavior. Ensure that your biases don't prevent you from being fair to each of your students.
- Attend events within your community that will help you learn more about students' cultures. I was recently at a workshop and some teachers reported that they volunteer to bag groceries at a local grocery store where many of the parents buy their food so they can meet and greet individuals within the community.
- Ensure that the materials, posters, and bulletin boards in your classroom reflect the diversity in today's society.

- Ensure that the instructional activities in your classroom build on the strengths of the student based on her or his culture. As an example, Ford and Kea (2009) discuss Afro-centric teaching and include the characteristics of movement and harmony. Sample strategies that incorporate these characteristics might include creative movement, mime, dance, and drama.
- Utilize the expertise of your students and their families to learn more about the cultures of the students within your classroom. One of the activities that I like to do to learn more about the culture of my students is to give each of them an empty paper bag. I then assign them to go home and collect some significant cultural artifacts that describe their family. They can bring in what they determine are the cultural artifacts that tell a story about their family. I also bring in my own bag and explain about my culture, and the students then do the same. I have discovered some wonderful information that has truly educated me about my students. Taylor and Bunte (1993) had high school students research their surnames and backgrounds and share the information with others. They also did activities that covered topics such as family gatherings, traditions, family stories, and cultural rituals. Such activities build a better awareness and respect of each student's culture. Time can then be spent discussing similarities and differences among differing cultures.
- Recognize that your expectations for the classroom may be different from the expectations that the child has at home. Behaviors that may be acceptable at home are not always acceptable at school, but it is important to respect the expectations at home and not degrade them. However, even though the child may be allowed to engage in a behavior at home, the child must be taught what is and what is not acceptable at school, as well as in some settings but not in other settings. If a student engages in behavior that is not acceptable at school, the teacher must pause and ask himself or herself—have I taught the student the appropriate behavior?

CHOICES OF TYPES OF ASSIGNMENTS AS AN EFFECTIVE BEHAVIORAL ADAPTATION

From an early age, students need to learn decision-making skills. They also want opportunities to have power and control. Building choice making into the classroom teaches both decision-making skills and gives students power and control. From an early age, children try to exert their own independence. While they can't have independence in some things, they certainly can be provided with the opportunity to be independent within the classroom. Choice making increases the likelihood that the student accepts ownership in the learning process and therefore increases the chance that the student will complete the task that the teacher has requested. With young students, the teacher will want to start by providing two choices to a student—otherwise students who have not been given choices previously will be overwhelmed by too many choices. After students have been provided with many opportunities for choice, then activities that build in more choices can be incorporated into the student's day.

The following are thirteen ideas for building choice into academic activities.

1. The student may choose to complete an assignment with a red pen or a blue pen, or a pencil or a pen.

2. The student may decide where to do the assignment—at the desk or at the round table in the room.

3. The student may complete a writing assignment on the computer or in handwriting.

4. The student may have the choice of completing the odd numbered or the even numbered problems.

5. Out of a set of twenty questions or problems, the student can choose any ten to complete.

6. Given two or three assignments to complete, the student can choose the order in which they are completed.

7. The student may choose whether to complete a creative writing assignment by writing down his or her thoughts or by saving those thoughts on a tape recorder.

8. The student has the choice of working alone and then having a break with time from the teacher or working with teacher assistance (Peterson, Caniglia, & Royster, 2001).

9. The student may choose the type of assignment to complete—a standard worksheet, a true and false test, or a game about the topic.

10. Instead of a worksheet following a lecture, the teacher can provide the student a tic-tac-toe sheet (see discussion of tic-tac-toe in Chapter 4) that includes nine possible alternative assignments, such as writing a skit, making a game, creating a word find, or drawing a picture. Students pick any three activities to complete to make a tic-tac-toe (Johns & Crowley, 2007). However, if you have not provided choices for children in the past, you will not want to begin with so many choices because students unaccustomed to making choices may be overwhelmed by so many. With young children in K–2, you will probably only want to provide two choices in any activity. You can also use tic-tac-toe as a test alternative.

11. Bingo can be used as a choice activity and lends itself to studying spelling words or answering problems. The teacher can give the student a bingo card with twenty-five different math problems or twenty-five vocabulary words or spelling words, and the student can pick five math problems, five spelling words to write a sentence about, or five vocabulary words to write their meanings. (See also discussion of bingo earlier in this chapter, as well as in Chapters 3 and 4.)

12. The teacher can buy and fill a small gum ball machine with variously colored gum balls (see Chapter 4). The color of the gum ball the student gets determines the assignment the student has to do.

13. For students who refuse to participate in a particular activity, teachers may want to consider integrating some optional activities during the school day, allowing some students to opt out of the assigned activity to do something different. As an example, I give older students a list of optional activities that they can do to get additional points, but they can opt not to do them.

SELF-MANAGEMENT STRATEGIES

Our goal is to teach all of our students to become independent individuals who can do and think for themselves. We are not always going to be around to control their behavior, so we need to teach our students to control their own behavior. A phenomenon in special education that has increased over the years is the use of one-on-one paraprofessionals. While those individuals can provide much needed assistance to students, we must be very careful that our students with special needs are not becoming too dependent on them. The one-on-one paraprofessional must provide needed assistance to the student, but also must be reinforcing the student for doing work independently.

A big advantage of teaching students how to manage their own behavior is that we are giving them control of their own lives—we are putting them in charge of their own behavior. Therefore such strategies will be reinforcing and motivating to students. We also are allowing them to see their own progress and reflect on what they can do differently. Many self-management strategies can be used with children. The important thing for the teacher to remember is the importance of incorporating those strategies into adaptations for students. Teachers can ask themselves the following questions to determine if they are teaching their students to become independent individuals.

- As a teacher, do I teach my students to control their own behaviors or am I spending a great deal of time controlling their behavior?

- As a teacher, do I encourage and reinforce my students' independence?
- Can my students list their strengths and deficits, as well as the accommodations they need?
- Do I engage in daily goal setting with my students?
- Do I model think-alouds with my students? That is, do I think out loud about the process used to get an answer or summarize the information learned? (The use of think-alouds is also discussed in Chapter 11.)
- Have I taught my students how to use mnemonics?
- Have I taught my students specific learning strategies?
- Do I provide opportunities for my students to experiment with their preferences for specific skills, like note taking and using assignment notebooks?
- Can my students act as their own advocates by articulating their own needs and their specific disability and what it means?
- Have I taught my students stress-reducing activities?
- Do my students know how to chart their own progress?
- Have I instilled in my students a sense of hope?
- Have I taught my students how to reinforce themselves and celebrate their successes?
- Do my students know about the power of reflection?
- Have I provided multiple opportunities throughout the day for choice-making activities?

Vanderbilt (2005) suggests that self-monitoring works well for decreasing off-task behavior and works best during individual seatwork and small group instruction.

How can the teacher incorporate self-management when working with students in the classroom? The teacher must work with the student to identify any behavior that is problematic, such as being out of the seat at inappropriate times. The teacher can then prepare a small chart that the student can keep on the desk. The chart states the opposite, positive behavior—the student is in her or his seat. The chart also is divided into short time segments such as five, ten, or fifteen minutes. If you are working with a young student, you will want to start with a five minute period. With an older student you may have ten or fifteen minutes, depending on the maturity level of the student. At the end of each time segment, the teacher signals the student to mark on the chart whether he or she is in the seat and then reinforces the student. This continues every few minutes, depending on the amount of time the teacher has decided. At the end of the morning, the teacher reviews the self-management chart with the student and reinforces the student for the number of correct marks. Eventually the teacher can wait until the end of the day, but must remember that students need frequent feedback. If the student puts a checkmark inappropriately, the teacher will have to meet with the student individually to correct the checkmark.

The student can then graph the number of checkmarks each day and see the improvement firsthand.

A number of other self-management strategies can be used. Daily goal setting is one. The student writes down a goal for the day, and at the end of the morning or at the end of the day the student can check whether the goal has been met.

Proofreading

A proofreading checklist is also a type of self-management tool. The teacher requests that before the student turns in an assignment, a proofreading checklist is completed: have I remembered to put my name on my paper, have I checked to make sure I have completed all the answers, have I used the correct punctuation? Some teachers make stamps of the proofreading checklist and stamp the right-hand corner of the assignment. Some teachers staple a proofreading checklist to the specific assignment.

Calming Strategies

Many adults spend a significant amount of money engaging in activities that are stress reducing and learning about techniques that reduce stress. We need to teach children at an early age stress-reduction activities so they can acquire those coping skills that will aid them throughout school and into their adult lives. Activities such as breathing deeply or counting to ten slowly reinforce themselves, and exercise as a stress reducer is important for students to learn.

Self-Monitoring Progress

Children love to see their own progress. They want to see how they are growing in their skills. For students who are working on their behavior or their academics, you can have them create graphs of the number of spelling words or the number of math facts they have mastered. A high school student who is learning a foreign language can chart the number of new words learned. Students also can graph their appropriate behavior— you may be working on teaching the student to raise a hand when she or he has a question. You can have the student self-monitor the behavior, and with each raising of the hand, another mark is added. Then the student can make a graph of the number of times he or she remembered to raise a hand.

Dot-to-dots also can be used to chart progress. The student can be supplied with a dot-to-dot sheet, and each time the student engages in the appropriate behavior he or she gets to draw a line from one dot to the next, with the goal being to connect all the dots to see what the picture is.

Avoid having students compete with each other with academics. For example, publicly posting the number of spelling words that each student in the class has mastered should be avoided. Those students who are poor spellers will feel overwhelmed because they don't see any way they can catch up with the great speller in the class. However, if students are charting their progress against themselves and not others, other students will be more likely to assist them because they have not been pitted against each other and see no need to compete.

Summary: Just 3×5 It

1. Effective preventive interventions include clear and positive expectations, precorrection, proximity, antiseptic bouncing, and behavior momentum.

2. Increasing our use of positive reinforcement through behavior-specific praise and attributions improves behavior.

3. Educators should monitor their own use of positive reinforcement through a variety of strategies like audiotaping, pennies in your pocket, bingo, or positive notes.

4. Fun ways to reinforce appropriate behavior include tickets and mystery motivators.

5. Interest-based interventions include the Nintendo effect and the Premack principle.

6. Effective behavioral interventions are based on students' strengths and are culturally responsive.

7. Building in a variety of choices is an effective behavioral adaptation.

8. Our goal is to teach our students to become independent and to monitor their own behavior.

6

Environmental
Adaptations

Recently I heard an individual with high-functioning autism talk about the horrible feeling that she experienced when she entered a building with fluorescent lighting. She said it was torture for her. Many times, unknowingly, we create an environment that is hostile to the student and we may not even realize we have done so. While many of us can adapt to fluorescent lighting or an unpleasant smell in the room, some children with autism, obsessive compulsive disorder, or ADHD cannot adapt to an environment that is unpleasant to them. They will fixate on something and it may ruin their day. All of us have experienced a room that was too warm or too cold and we could not learn as well because we were not at our optimal level of alertness. Learners may have sensory-based needs that require heightened sensory input or diminished sensory input. The student then becomes a sensory seeker, an underresponder, or an overresponder to environmental stimuli (Murray, Baker, Murray-Slutsky, & Paris, 2009).

In a class I visited recently, the teacher wanted to make sure that the students were given many visual cues for spelling words, meanings of vocabulary words, math facts, grammar facts, and on and on. As a result, she had posters of different grammar or math facts covering almost every inch of wall space. So much information was posted that I couldn't take it all in. The room was too visually overwhelming and distracting. Students had difficulty pulling out key information because there was so much of it. While we want to have visual cues around the room, the teacher can provide so much that the student cannot process it all.

Planning an appropriate classroom environment is critical to the success of the students, and this chapter focuses on how to do that.

THE CLASSROOM ENVIRONMENT

Bringing Beauty Into the Environment

Many years ago I wrote an article, *Making School a Place to Call Home* (Johns, 1997). In that article I talked about the importance of beauty in the environment, a critical point to me. We send a message to our students by the type of environment that we create for them—that message is that we care so much about you that we want our environment to be a beautiful place where you want to be. I have often told my students that I dress up to teach classes because "I believe that you are so important that I want to look my best for you." The same philosophy applies to the school and classroom environment. When I wrote that article, I received a number of comments about it. Many individuals thought the ideas were good for elementary schools but that high schools did not have to be beautiful environments because high school students wouldn't notice. I found that indeed they did. All of us want to enter environments where there is beauty and it is a pleasant and clean place to be. What kind of message do we send to students when we have a dirty building with broken windows and paint peeling? Why is beauty in the environment a critical adaptation for students with special needs? Some of our students bring a great deal of negative emotional baggage to school. School has been difficult for them and they may not want to be there because they perceive the school environment as one of failure. If a physical environment is created that is warm and friendly in appearance, the students may feel more comfortable in that environment.

One of my early classrooms of kindergarten students took place in a room with a real fountain. That fountain added so much beauty and comfort to the room. When I was the administrator of an alternative school for students with significant behavioral disorders, I created a school where there were silk plants, carpeting, and bright pictures throughout the building. There were cozy sitting areas at the entrances to the building so people would feel welcome right away. Students could also sit and read in a courtyard with a garden.

Since I wrote that original article, I have found more schools creating warm welcoming environments that are beautiful places to be—unlike some of the sterile, institutional environments that existed at one time.

The following are ideas for adding beauty to the school and classroom environment.

- Place silk plants throughout the building or classroom. If you have a green thumb, you may want to have real plants and have the students accept responsibility for watering and feeding them.
- Cover the fluorescent lights with a drape or paint a picture on the tiles with the lights. Or include lamps in the classroom. I was recently in a classroom where the teacher had about seven lamps around the room and she did not have the fluorescent lights on at all—it really made the classroom look warm and cozy. Even if the fluorescent lights are on, one or two lamps will soften the light. Teachers can have students read in an area with a lamp—the lamp is more conducive to reading and the light can assist the child in focusing on the printed page.
- Use curtains. I have seen schools that have decorated the doors to their classrooms with curtains. This really adds a homey atmosphere. Bright curtains can be added to the windows in the classroom as well.
- Incorporate round tables. In a home, people tend to congregate around the kitchen table. Tables are conducive to work and round tables are even more so. More schools are now putting round tables in their cafeterias to remove the institutional feel of long tables. I remember a teacher who put a tablecloth on the round table in her room. Her students had the choice of working at the round table with the tablecloth or working at their desks. Many students chose the round table.
- Include carpeted areas. Even though the entire classroom may not be carpeted, many teachers add carpet squares or an area rug to diffuse noise and to make the classroom seem more homey and welcoming to the students. My favorites are carpets with built-in learning, such as those with the numbers on it or a map of the United States.
- Have one or more rocking chairs available. Rockers allow movement and are comforting to some students. They also provide a homey feeling in the room. (There's more on the use of rockers in Chapter 7.)
- Include couches, comfortable chairs, or beanbag chairs. Couches and beanbag chairs are increasingly popular in classrooms. If the teacher has a large enough classroom, a couch or a couple of comfortable chairs and a lamp or two can create a nice reading area. This is much more inviting to students than reading at their desks.
- Add small fountains. As I mentioned earlier, I was fortunate enough to have a classroom one time that had a fountain in it. It was very calming to the students. Now, small portable fountains are available from many sources.

- Hang photos or paintings. I have found that students love to look at pictures of themselves. To get parents to come to open house, I used to take family pictures. I would make one copy for the family and put another copy in a photo album in the school. I put the photo albums out where students could look at them. My students loved this. Of course, motivational posters or pictures add to the décor of the classroom. I once found an artist who painted a large depiction of the United States, the solar system, our state, and the world. I placed those on the cafeteria walls and in the hallways. Since they were done with bright colors, the students loved to look at them and activities were planned to study what was in the paintings.

When planning for changes in the environment, be sure to check with your building administrator to determine whether any fire and safety codes may prohibit certain items.

Organizing the Environment

Our students are looking for structure and order in their lives, so it is important that the environment be well organized and maintained. Items should be kept in their designated spaces. Children should know where everything belongs and be taught to put everything back when they are finished with it. Teachers can label where items should be placed to assist students in knowing where to return items. In a cluttered place, children can become overwhelmed. When there is too much in the classroom, the teacher or the students may be unable to find what they need and instructional time is lost in the process.

We have all encountered students whose desks are an absolute mess, with items falling all over the place if the desk has open storage, or the student opens the lid to the desk and can't find anything because papers are all over the place. One solution to this problem is to have the student or students put their items in plastic tubs (this is also discussed in Chapter 7). The students can keep all of their books and papers in the tubs, which are kept in another part of the classroom. When math is finished, they can go to their plastic tub, put the math away, and get out the next subject. This also provides students with the opportunity to move.

Students should be taught to clean out on a regular basis, so it is preferable to spend a little time each day devoted to going through papers and throwing away what is not needed. This creates a habit for the student— spending time at the end of every day to clean up and organize materials.

Some teachers color code materials and provide different colored files for different subjects—green might be math and would be placed in a green file folder, red would be reading, and so on.

We also may have encountered students who are very particular about their work space and don't want anything out of order. One of my colleagues worked with a student with obsessive compulsive disorder and the student became very upset when any of his papers from different subjects touched each other. The teacher went out and bought the student his own personal cardboard mailbox with nine different slots so that he could organize his papers and put different subjects in different slots.

Using Aromas and Foods

A number of teachers use air fresheners in their classroom—this may be necessary in classes with middle school males. Air fresheners with specific fragrances may be very pleasant to the majority of students but the teacher must make sure that no student in the classroom is allergic to the chosen fragrance. I was in a classroom recently where a high school boy wreaked of strong-smelling cologne. It caused a seizure in one of the staff members. We must be cognizant that certain smells may evoke a seizure for a student. Neutral air fresheners can be used when necessary.

I like to have students associate certain activities with pleasant food smells. For example, the teacher could pop popcorn and let students eat part and have them do manipulative math with popcorn kernels. You can use pizza or vegetable soup to teach the parts of speech—when the ingredients are put together, they make a sentence.

When bringing food to the classroom, know the specific dietary needs of your students. Some students cannot have sugar, chocolate, or nuts. Some students require diets that must be wheat-free and gluten-free. One teacher reported that the smell of popcorn resulted in a migraine for a student.

Preparing Students for Changes in the Environment

I have known teachers who like to rearrange their room frequently. Some change the room around over the weekend so when the students come in on Monday morning they are surprised. This may be a fun surprise for some students, but can be very bothersome for students who don't adapt well to change. It may be upsetting to a student with autism, Asperger Syndrome, or obsessive compulsive disorder. Prior to changing the room arrangement, the teacher must think very carefully about the impact of the change on each student.

An alternative approach is to involve the students in the classroom environment change. The teacher might seek the students' input and may actually have them help with the room change. That way no surprise is involved and students feel a sense of ownership.

Some students with special needs may even notice very small changes we make in the environment that we think they wouldn't even see.

Always prepare the students for those changes and share the reason the change was made.

Desensitizing the Student to Noise in the Environment

Some students have difficulty coping with the noise in the cafeteria or in an assembly. I remember working with a student who hated to go to assemblies where music was played. I can still remember him saying, "No Jingle Bells" when we were scheduled to have holiday assemblies. What we did was to take him to the environment before the other students arrived and have him sit near the back of the large room. The other students arrived, and we had him stay in the assembly for a just short time—perhaps five minutes—before we took him away. The next time, we had him stay in the assembly a little longer, and the next time even longer, so he got used to the environment slowly.

For some students, headphones can block out some of the noise within the classroom.

It is critical to know the background of the student when planning activities in which noise can be a factor. I worked with a young lady whose mother popped a balloon in the young lady's ear when she was young, terrifying her. So, we avoided parties with balloons because she would become very upset and hover in a corner, even as a young adult.

Creating a Quiet Place for the Student

A common intervention for students with autism in today's schools is the designation of a safe place where the child can go when he or she is upset to be alone or with another adult. These are necessary for many of our students—we can request that they go to a quiet area when we see they are growing upset about something. Usually the teacher decides when the student can go to the quiet place, but the student also can be taught to ask to go for a short time to regain self-control.

Incorporating Music Into the Environment

I am a lover of music and use it in the classroom every chance I get, regardless of the age of the student. There is some research about the impact of music on various skills of students with special needs. As early as 1953, Schneider showed improvements in motor skills, attention, and the relaxation of students with cerebral palsy. Kiger (1989) showed the positive impact of various types of music on high school students' performance of reading.

I always play music when I do training with adults. One evening, the equipment to play music was not available, so I couldn't use it. Some of the evaluations had comments such as "We really missed the music." The following are some of the many ways to incorporate music into the environment.

- Play soft music to calm students.
- Have fun music playing when the students arrive in the morning. The music can be something that teases the students about an activity that they face that day. Play music that is designed to teach. A number of companies publish music designed for learning the colors, the alphabet, or math facts.
- Use songs to teach spelling words or other subject content. For example, "Row, Row, Row Your Boat" can be used to teach five-letter spelling words that may be difficult for the student. Students use the tune to spell out a difficult word, such as *spent*. I know someone who created a song to teach the prepositions to the tune of "Yankee Doodle Dandy."
- Have the students write a song about a topic that is being studied.
- Use the theme songs from the games you like to play in the classroom—*Wheel of Fortune, Who Wants to Be a Millionaire, Jeopardy*. It makes the game even more fun to introduce it with the theme song.
- Use music associated with your activities. When I play Red Rubber Ball (discussed in Chapter 2), I play the music associated with it, an old song called "Red Rubber Ball" recorded by The Cyrkle (Simon & Woodley, 1966). When I engage the students in a carousel brainstorming activity (see Chapters 4 and 7), I play the Beach Boys song "I Get Around" (Wilson & Love, 1964).
- When students transition or line up for an activity, try marching music.
- Allow students to listen to certain music on headphones, if it assists them in learning.
- Use music as part of the Premack principle (discussed in Chapter 5). The student who works at an activity for a specified period then receives time to listen to music.
- For students who have long bus rides and tend to have behavioral problems on the bus, allow them to listen to music on their headphones. This can keep them busy so they don't engage in problem behaviors.
- Use music for physical activities. We must get our students up and moving as much as possible, though some students are reluctant exercisers. Music may motivate them to exercise.

A word of caution about music in the classroom: the teacher must listen to the music first to check that it contains no inappropriate comments or anything that may be upsetting to the student. I am reminded of a classroom of young students in which the teacher was playing a funny song about a mother. The night before, one of the children had been removed from his home when his mother was put in jail. He was having a very rough day and, when the song about a mother came on, he started crying—it was too hard for him to deal with this song.

SUMMARY: A THERAPEUTIC ENVIRONMENT

"Therapeutic teachers create a positive classroom environment in which students experience success and feel safe" (Abrams, 2005, p. 40). Creating that positive environment requires that educators establish a caring relationship by showing genuine interest in their students, demonstrating to the student that the teacher wants that student to achieve, and conveying frequent positive statements when the student is successful. Such an environment includes beauty, which conveys to the students that they are important and deserve a place that is physically, socially, and emotionally appealing.

Summary: Just 3×5 It

1. A classroom environment that provides beauty instills in students that school is a place where they are wanted and valued.

2. Beauty in the environment also can evoke a sense of comfort for students.

3. Educators should provide structure and order in classrooms so that students know exactly what is expected of them and feel a sense of security.

4. Educators may create a classroom aroma that is pleasant for students but should ensure that the smell in the room will not cause an allergic reaction or a seizure.

5. Educators may involve students in any change in the classroom environment. Educators can create unnecessary anxiety for students who are surprised with a change in the environment. Classrooms should be fear-free.

6. Educators must adapt for students who are sensitive to noise by avoiding unnecessary loud noises and preparing students for loud noises that are not preventable.

7. Music may be incorporated into learning in multiple ways. Music that is associated with the specific activity or music that is used for transitions can be helpful and motivating for the student.

8. Classrooms should be designed to be safe and welcoming for students.

7

Movement Adaptations

"**I** can't let him move around because he gets too excited and then I can't get him calmed down." These words are often voiced by teachers who have students with ADHD within their classrooms. It is a realistic fear; yet students with ADHD are really telling us that they need movement and activity in order to learn. If we don't allow them movement, they may not be learning and then become disruptive.

Some teachers penalize students who act up in class by denying them recess or physical education time. This is an ineffective intervention for many students because they need an outlet for their energy. If they don't have that outlet, they may act up even more. We want to encourage our students to be active and engaged learners, and movement is an integral part of that engagement.

Movement also provides an outlet for exercise for many students, not just students with ADHD. With the common use of technology, many of our children have become couch potatoes, and thus we have a major problem today with obesity in children. Movement is critical for students to be engaged in the learning process, and it is also critical to ensure that students get the needed exercise, along with a healthy diet.

Movement can also encourage social skills in our children. Students who are engaged in activities are more likely to interact with other students socially. Positive social interactions set the stage for getting along with others—a key factor in promoting job skills in today's society. This chapter provides tools that allow movement without disruption and provides activity-based interventions that incorporate movement. It also provides some ideas on how to divide students into groups.

TOOLS THAT ALLOW MOVEMENT WITHOUT DISRUPTION

Occasionally I hear teachers say that they don't allow doodling within their classroom because they want the students' undivided attention. The flip side of that is that the student may be unable to attend unless the student is allowed to doodle. Haven't we all gone to meetings and seen a participant knitting while the leader is talking? Some leaders become insulted; yet on further observation, these participants are interacting, asking questions, and responding to key points. Knitting seems to help them concentrate.

Fidgets

Students can use a variety of fidgets to relieve their stress. It may be a squeeze ball, an item that twists, or a small pack of play dough. It may be a pencil grip. A fidget is an item that will keep the students' hands busy and allow them to channel their stress or their energy by playing with the item. You also can have students make their own fidgets. Get some cheap hair gel and small plastic bags with ties from a dollar store. The students can put the hair gel into the bags and tie them, creating their own fidget. I always recommend that the teacher keep a supply of fidgets in the classroom so that students can choose which type works best for them.

Doodle Pads

Rather than having natural doodlers mark in their notebooks, give them a notepad or notebook specifically for doodling.

Seat Cushion or Exercise Ball

We all know individuals who can't sit still in their seats—perhaps we were those individuals. I found it interesting recently that a bank president reported that he had been asked by an adult who worked at a desk job whether she could have one of the large exercise balls as her seat rather than the standard desk chair. He was very agreeable to do so. Some schools are making the exercise balls available to students to use as their seat, rather than their standard desk chair.

We can make a number of adaptations within the classroom to meet these students' needs. Teachers can purchase a type of seat cushion that allows the student to shift in the seat. As mentioned in Chapter 2, a cheap way to accomplish this is to purchase a beach ball and partially inflate it for use as a seat cushion.

Mouse Pad for Tapping the Pencil

Some students like to tap a pencil on the desk, which may be very bothersome to the teacher or to other students. An easy intervention for this is to supply the student with a mouse pad on which the student can tap so the sound will be diffused. The teacher also can have a mouse pad printed with key facts that students are studying; that way the student has easy access to critical information while using the mouse pad to tap.

Licorice or Fruit Rollup for Chewing on a Pencil or Pen

I learned this trick from one of my college students, who had been allowed to do this in high school. The student had chewed on her pencil during class. At this time, pencils still contained lead, so one of them decided to roll a fruit rollup around the pencil. That way the student could chew on the rollup rather than the pencil.

Another option is a stick of licorice wrapped around the pencil. I have heard some educators say that students should not be allowed to suck on sugar—I admit I have my concerns—but I would rather the student be allowed to suck on some sugar than on a dirty pencil or lead.

Exercise Pedal Under the Desk

Some students just have to keep their feet moving while they sit at their desk. An exercise pedal is good for these students. They can be purchased for about $10 and were designed to allow people to exercise while seated. Put the pedal under the student's desk and the student can pedal while working, and the pedal does not disrupt other students.

Exercise Bicycle or Treadmill in the Classroom

I got this idea from a young lady with whom I was fortunate enough to work. She has Prader-Willi syndrome and is quite obese, so she needed as much exercise as possible while in her special education classroom. Her parents asked if it would be possible to have an exercise bicycle within the classroom. We were very willing to accommodate this request and acquired one. When we wanted her to exercise, we asked her to ride the bicycle and read a book—she liked to read books. It wasn't long before other students asked if they also could ride the bicycle while they read. So a schedule was worked out. We also found another location for a treadmill, which was donated and allowed students to read while they walked.

Whether the student can read while on a bicycle or a treadmill certainly will depend on the student and his or her motor skills. I've seen a number of individuals at my health club who read books while on the treadmill or the bike. However, it doesn't work for me because my motor skills are not strong—while on the bike or the treadmill I need to concentrate on the exercise because I am afraid I might lose my balance. Therefore my reading comprehension is poor because I am so worried that I might fall. You likely will have students as uncoordinated as I am and will face the same problem.

A Podium at Which to Stand When Working

We tend to think that all students have to be seated to complete assignments. Some students, however, may work better while standing. An alternative for those students is to work at a podium. Put it on a desk or table and let the student stand while working.

Rockers for Reading

I love to go into libraries and see rocking chairs around for people to use. I also am seeing rockers in some airports for people to use while they wait. Many of us like to rock and find it very comforting. Students can sit in the rocking chair while they read—for some the movement results in better attention. Rockers are not just appropriate for young students but can be very effective for older students as well.

In the early days of working with children with autism, a great deal of time was spent trying to get them to quit rocking back and forth. Now we have learned to capitalize on the fact that they like to rock and build in academics while they do so.

Plastic Tubs for Storage

I have known a number of teachers who provide a plastic tub for each student in which to place all of her or his work and books. The tubs are marked and are kept away from each student's desk. The students keep nothing at their desk except what they are working with at the time. When it is time for English, the student takes whatever he or she was working on before and puts it in the tub. Then the English work comes out and the student brings it back to the desk. When English is over, the student goes over to the tub and puts that material away and gets out what is needed for the next class. This helps keep the student organized. It also builds in the opportunity for movement after each class.

Two or More Different Work Areas

Teachers who have large enough classrooms may have adequate space for some students to have two different work areas. The student might work at the desk for one subject but then work at a round table for another subject. The student may want to work at a table for one class but prefers a study carrel for another assignment.

Built-In Movement Breaks

Movement breaks are important for students of all ages. How often those movement breaks should occur will depend not only on the age of the student but also the level of activity the student requires. Recently I was in two classrooms of primary age students. In one classroom, the students worked on an assignment in one area of the room; after five minutes they were directed by the teacher or the assistant to another activity in another part of the room. This continued for an hour, and students were well-engaged because activities were switched often and the students got to move around.

In the other classroom, the teacher had the students move from one activity to another in a different part of the room every fifteen minutes. I was in the classroom for two hours and the time flew. The students had few behavioral issues (even though it was a class for students with significant behavioral problems).

Even with older students, we need to build in movement breaks. The students might work at something for fifteen minutes and then move from one work area to another or get their pencil sharpened.

Walk and Learn

This is a good activity for older students. The teacher can lecture for a short time—five to seven minutes—and then the students can be instructed to work with a partner (see the section on breaking students into groups later in this chapter for ideas on how to choose partners). To work with their partner, they must take a short walk around the room or, if supervision is available, they can go out in the hall with their partner to discuss the three most important points they learned.

Music With Movement

Students can sing a song about math facts or spelling words, and at the end of certain verses or when a certain word is heard in the song, they stand up.

ACTIVITY-BASED INTERVENTIONS THAT ENCOURAGE MOVEMENT

Dominoes

I love to play my version of the dominoes game with students (it is also discussed in Chapters 2 and 8). One variation is to prepare a set of index cards with key vocabulary words being studied on one card and the definition printed on another card. Make enough cards for each student in the class. The teacher then shuffles the deck of cards and distributes one to each student. Students then move around the room to find their match. When all of the students have found their match, the students then share their word and definition with the rest of the class. Another variation of this game is to prepare a set of four cards per category. The students then have to find the cards that go together. For instance, the class might be studying states and their cities. The teacher would put cities that are in certain states on cards and students have to find the classmates who also have cities from that particular state.

Traveling Assignment

The traveling assignment is described in Chapter 4 on worksheet adaptations, and it is an excellent activity for a student with ADHD. Essentially the student's worksheet is cut into several strips. Those strips are posted around the room and the student, carrying a clipboard, goes to each section, looks at the questions, and writes the answers on a clipboard.

Shower Curtain or Plastic Tablecloth on the Floor

It is fun, particularly for young students, to allow them to answer questions by moving to the answer that is printed on a shower curtain or plastic tablecloth (also discussed in Chapter 4). The teacher can give the student a math problem or definition of a word and the student can move to the answer on the tablecloth or shower curtain. Learning rugs can be purchased when students are learning their letters of the alphabet or numbers. Some rugs show the map of the United States; students can move to the appropriate state on the map.

Carousel Brainstorming

This is one of my favorite activities for building movement into activities (also described in Chapter 4) and it can be done in several ways. This activity is appropriate for students from fourth grade through high school and I have used it in workshops with adults to generate many ideas. The music that I use for this activity is "I Get Around" by the Beach Boys (Wilson & Love, 1964).

One way the teacher can use this technique is to pose five different problem situations—for example, social skills problems that might be occurring within the classroom. The teacher writes five different situations on large flip chart paper and places the pages around the room. Then the students are divided into groups (see the section later in this chapter on breaking students into groups). Each group is assigned to begin at a specific location where one of the pieces of flip chart paper is posted. When the music begins, groups move to their first location. One student, designated as the recorder, writes down as many solutions to the problem as the group can generate. They continue for at least five or six minutes, depending on their grade level. When the music starts again, they move to the next problem. This process continues until each group has generated solutions to all of the problems that have been posted. The students then can move around and look at each solution and the teacher talks with the students about them. By the fourth and fifth stop at a paper station, the group may not require as much time as they did at the first one because they may be running out of ideas.

Here are some additional brainstorming options.

- The teacher can use the same format as explained previously except that on each sheet of paper, the teacher posts a vocabulary word that the students are studying. Each group can either give examples of the vocabulary word or write a sentence using the vocabulary word.
- If the class is studying a particular country, the teacher can post five different categories of information about the country—for instance, food from the country, cultural information, famous people from the country, geographic information, and weather information. The students then are responsible for listing all the information.
- Here is a fun way to review math information. The teacher provides math problems. The first group at a station has to solve that problem and then pose another one for the next group to solve.
- At each station, the teacher provides a topic for a story. The first group has to write the first sentence. The next group adds another sentence, and so forth. When the rounds are completed, there will be a five sentence story about the topic. It can be really fun to read the end products.

Carousel brainstorming activities can be varied with smaller groups of students and each student can begin at one of the stations and work independently while moving around as explained previously. Rather than having a student complete an entire worksheet of math problems, students can have their desks in a circle and each student is given the same math sheet. The first student completes the first three problems. When the music starts, the student passes the worksheet clockwise and answers the next three problems, and so forth. By the time the math sheet returns to the student, it is complete; yet the work was broken down into three problem segments.

Human Billboard

This is another one of my favorite activities, and it can be done in a couple of ways. The teacher can become a human billboard. It starts with key concepts about a topic added to the front side of a piece of poster board and more key facts on the side that will be worn on the teacher's back. The teacher then punches two holes at the top on both pieces of poster board. Pulling string through each of the holes and tying the string together makes the poster board wearable. I have used it to help students remember the rules of the classroom. I wear the rules on the front part of my billboard and put some key information that we are studying on the other side.

The teacher can have students make their own copy of a human billboard. Each student can be assigned a vocabulary word and they can make a graphic organizer on one side and give examples of the word on the other side. I have found that even high school students think this activity is fun, and it is certainly very appropriate for young students.

Puzzles

See Chapter 11, Note-Taking Adaptations, for an explanation on using puzzle forms for note taking. Another fun activity to do with students is to assign each one a vocabulary word. The teacher provides a blank sheet of paper that is divided into puzzle pieces. On each puzzle piece, the student has to write a clue about the word without using the word. The student then cuts the puzzle into pieces and puts the pieces in a small plastic bag. The teacher redistributes the bags to different students, who then have to put the puzzle pieces together and guess the word.

BREAKING STUDENTS INTO GROUPS

I am very sensitive about how teachers break students into groups because I remember very well how students were chosen to be on teams when I was growing up. My weaknesses in motor skills made me the child that nobody wanted on their softball or volleyball team. Team captains would always choose me last because I was not a good player. As an elementary student, this was traumatic. As I got older, it was a very embarrassing situation.

We must be very careful that we don't set up students for embarrassment. Here are some other ways of breaking students into groups.

Rock Around the Clock

The teacher makes individual sheets that have a circle divided into four parts, corresponding to twelve noon, three o'clock, six o'clock, and nine o'clock. The teacher assigns partners ahead of time and gives students appointments with other students. For instance, a student has a nine o'clock appointment with a student, a six o'clock appointment with a different student, and so forth. When it's time for students to work with partners, the teacher may tell them to work with their six o'clock appointment. The clock sheet can be updated periodically so that students get an opportunity to work with various students. The teacher can pair students with varying abilities as well.

A variation on this is to have the students walk around the room and make appointments for each time period.

The song I use for this activity is "Rock Around the Clock" (Freedman & Myers, 1952).

Categories

Depending on what the class is studying, the teacher can write down on index cards or small pieces of paper words in a given category and have students move around the room finding the students who have the words in the same category. The category members constitute a group.

Dominoes

This is appropriate if students will be working in pairs. The teacher can write a vocabulary word on an index card and a definition on another card. The students have to move around the room finding the student who has the match to their card and then the students are partners for an activity.

Types of Candy

Each student draws a piece of candy or gum out of a sack containing four or five different types. Students then break into groups according to the type of candy or gum they received, and at the end of the activity they get to eat the candy or chew the gum. Be careful about the use of candy if any students in your class have diabetes. You may want to use sugarless candy or gum.

Humdinger

This is a fun activity for students and also is a good listening and movement activity. Each of the students is given a sheet of paper that has the name of an easy song, such as "Jingle Bells," "Row, Row, Row Your Boat," or "Mary Had a Little Lamb." The students are instructed that they have to move around the room humming the song they were assigned and find the students who are humming the same song. Students humming the same song form a group.

Summary: Just 3×5 It

1. Educators should provide multiple opportunities for movement throughout the school day so students become more engaged in the learning process.

2. Movement provides exercise and encourages social skills.

3. Allow students to fidget and to doodle.

4. Provide opportunities for students to move in their seats with seat cushions or exercise balls, and to move their feet with pedals under their desk.

5. For students who like to chew on objects, provide licorice or a fruit rollup wrapped around their pencil.

6. Allow students to stand while working, have two different work areas, or to use an exercise bicycle or rocker while reading.

7. Activity-based interventions such as dominoes, traveling assignment, carousel brainstorming, or human billboard encourage movement.

8. Appropriate ways to break students into groups include rock around the clock, categories, or humdinger.

Vocabulary Adaptations

Vocabulary instruction is a key component in improving reading comprehension skills and is one of the five areas that are essential to reading instruction. Students who are good readers have large vocabularies that are nurtured by reading. When students with special needs such as learning disabilities avoid reading because it is difficult for them, they are limiting their exposure to vocabulary (Roberts, Torgesen, Boardman, & Scammacca, 2008). Most textbooks don't provide multiple opportunities for vocabulary learning (Hirsch, 2003). I frequently review social studies and science textbooks that provide the new vocabulary list for the student that accompanies the chapter. Yet when one reviews the chapters, one finds even more vocabulary words that may not be in the repertoire of the students, especially those students with special needs.

There is additional complexity for students with special needs in learning words that have multiple meanings—this will be a hard concept for students with cognitive disabilities, as well as for some students with learning disabilities. They understand one meaning of the word but have difficulty grasping that certain words like *note* have many meanings. If they don't understand this concept, it will impact their reading comprehension, as well as their conversations with individuals who may use the word in a context different than what the student has learned (Lerner & Johns, 2009).

Beck, McKeown, and Kucan (2002) recommend breaking vocabulary words into three tiers. Tier 1 includes those words that students are likely to know. Tier 2 includes words that appear frequently in many contexts. Tier 3 includes words that appear rarely or are content specific. The majority of instruction for students with special needs will focus on those Tier 2 words that they need to know. Some instruction will need to focus on Tier 3 words.

The acquisition of vocabulary is attained through the natural learning of word meanings while reading or through vocabulary instruction. For students with special needs, vocabulary acquisition is hindered by memory and language problems. Students with special needs also may be reluctant readers, so specific instruction on vocabulary words must occur (Fore, Boon, & Lowrie, 2007).

It has been found that as many as twelve exposures may be necessary to create a deep understanding of a new word (McKeown, Beck, Omanson, & Pople, 1985). Students with special needs will need even more exposures to words in order to develop their understanding and usage of the words.

This chapter includes a variety of ways to provide multiple opportunities for students with special needs to expand their vocabulary.

VOCABULARY ADAPTATIONS

Concept Diagrams

The traditional method of involving students in looking up and writing down definitions of words and using each word in a sentence is not the most effective way to teach students with special needs, particularly students with learning disabilities. Active involvement by creating concept diagrams is more effective. The concept diagram encompasses the vocabulary word itself, the definition, characteristics, and examples and nonexamples of the word. The teacher needs to model creating the graphic about the word, and then students can create their own models. In a study conducted by Fore, Boon, and Lowrie (2007), they found that students with learning disabilities learned words much better this way than using the traditional method. For example, if working with students to teach them about the word *broccoli*, we might have the box in the middle with the word *broccoli*. An arrow would go to another box that includes the definition as a food in the vegetable category that can be eaten cooked or uncooked. Another arrow would go to a box that talked about characteristics of broccoli, such as its green color and its hard texture. Another arrow would go to a box that gave nonexamples: not a fruit, not meat, and not eaten for dessert.

Word Webs

A word web is a graphic organizer and can be an effective strategy to teach students specific vocabulary words. A word web can enrich the associations with a word. The word web might include three questions: What is it? What is it like? And what are some examples (Lerner & Johns, 2009)?

Building on Past Experiences

New vocabulary words should be linked or associated with familiar words. The teacher must pull in the background knowledge that the student has in order to teach the vocabulary. I worked recently in a classroom with a student with cognitive disabilities. She loved horses and knew quite a bit about them, so we tried to connect some of the words she was learning with her experience with horses.

TEACHING THE USE OF VOCABULARY RESOURCES

Textbook Glossary

One of the first things a teacher ought to do, when introducing a new textbook in the classroom, is to teach students how to make use of the textbook. The student must know how to use the table of contents, the glossary, various tables in the book, and the questions at the end of the chapters. The teacher should spend time with students reviewing these features. I was in a classroom where a student with special needs had been assigned to look up specific vocabulary words. He paged through the chapter looking for the words and had no idea that there was a glossary in the book. I showed him the key parts of the book and had him mark those parts with sticky notes so he could easily find them.

Dictionary and Thesaurus

Teaching the use of the dictionary to students with special needs can be difficult. Such students can be overwhelmed by the size of the dictionary, they may not know how to alphabetize, and if they can't spell they will have trouble finding the word and its meaning. The teacher will need to do a number of activities together with the students: scavenger hunts, working on one letter of the alphabet at first, and double-checking to make sure the student knows the spelling of a word. Many teachers work with students to use the spell-check feature of a word processing program, but remember that may not always be successful.

The teacher should also show the student how to electronically search for a word using an online dictionary and its meaning and synonyms. An activity that may be of interest and helpful to some students is to do both—an electronic search for the meaning of the word or a synonym from an online thesaurus and then have the student use the hard copy dictionary and thesaurus. Students can then compare and contrast the differences between the findings from these different sources. Some of the new electronic books allow readers to click on a word that they don't know the meaning of and the definition will appear. Phenomenal things are happening in the world of electronic books.

Vocabulary Games

Dominoes

As mentioned in the previous chapter, I like to do this activity with a group of students. I write words on some index cards and their definitions on others. The students then have to walk around the room and find the student whose card matches theirs.

Password

Password is an old game but is a fun one for teaching vocabulary. One person is given a word and has to give clues one word at a time until the other person can guess the word. This can be done with a team as well.

"I'm Thinking of a Word That . . ."

The teacher can begin by offering clue about a word. If any student guesses the word after one clue, that student receives ten points. If no one guesses the word, the teacher provides another clue. Any student who guesses the word then would get nine points. And the game continues in that vein. This can either be played with an individual or as a team game. The teacher should carefully orchestrate the teams so they are as evenly matched as possible. This is a good game for older students.

Concentration/Memory

I love this game (see Chapter 4) because it can be played at school and the children also can take the game home and practice the words. A set of cards with the important vocabulary words being studied is made. One word is printed on an index card, the definition on another. Or each student can make a set of the words and their definitions. The cards can be put in a baggie for easy transport.

Charades

In this game, the students act out the word and the other students then try to guess what it is. There can then be a discussion of the meaning of the word.

Hide and Seek

For this game, the teacher can hide three or four words around the room for the students to find. When each word is found, students look up the word in the dictionary.

Scavenger Hunt

This is another fun activity to do with the dictionary. The teacher can provide each student a picture and the student has to find the word in the dictionary that names what's in the picture.

Vocabulary Name Tags

This classroom activity is fun for students up to the fourth grade. The teacher determines the vocabulary words to be learned. Each day when the students enter, they are given a name tag to wear all day. That name tag doesn't have the student's name on it—instead it has a vocabulary word the students are learning. Each student is responsible for looking up the definition of the vocabulary word and becoming as familiar as possible with the word. They are responsible for sharing with the class what the word means. Because students wear the name tag all day, they can be stopped by teachers or other support personnel within the building and questioned about the word.

Vocabulary Footprints

This is a fun activity that involves movement. The teacher sticks footprints on the floor making a trail. Each footprint has a vocabulary word on it and, as the students move, they name the word and explain what the word means (Morgan & Moni, 2007).

Multisensory Approach

Many students require a multisensory approach to learning new vocabulary words. Once a vocabulary word is introduced to the student, younger students can trace the word in sand or shaving cream. The teacher can make sandpaper words; that is, each of the letters is made with sandpaper and the student can feel the word. Then the students can practice tracing their fingers over the letter while saying the word, and then the teacher can review the meaning of the word.

Older students can type vocabulary words—sometimes students remember the word better if they have had the tactile involvement with the word. A number of computer programs have voice-text so the student can both see and hear the word.

To illustrate the word and its meaning, the teacher should show a picture of what the word names, if possible, or bring in the actual object. For instance, if the word is *asparagus,* the teacher can bring in asparagus to show.

Rather than having the student write the definition of the word, the student can write the name of the word on one side of an index card and on the other side of the card they can draw a picture or a graphic organizer that helps them remember the meaning of the word.

Some words may be depicted by demonstration. If the word is *alienation,* the teacher can role play two people separated from each other.

To expand the multisensory approach, students can make a product that depicts the particular word.

The more senses involved in teaching the word, the better.

Word Banks

In the first chapter of this book, I include an example of the use of a word bank being recommended for a particular student, as well as the classroom teacher who did not understand that term. A word bank is a collection of words available to the student for use for a particular activity. For a test with fill-in the blanks, a list of the words that are to be used to fill in the blanks is provided to the students. For a test, the students may be given a word bank if there are questions that involve the use of the words. For a unit of study, the word bank contains key words that are related to the topic and are important for the student to understand to learn the content (Borgia, Owles, & Beckler, 2007). Word banks are important for students with special needs because they provide a prompt for the student to use to either figure out an answer or to recognize the important words within the unit of study.

Card File or Rolodex

The teacher may encourage students to keep their vocabulary words on index cards with the word on one side and the definition and a depiction of that definition on the other side. The students can then keep the vocabulary words in a card file or in a rolodex. This is important for older students who are involved in several content area classes.

Summary: Just 3×5 It

1. Up to twelve exposures of a word and its meaning may be needed to create a deep understanding of the word's meaning—even more exposures to the word will be needed for some of our students with special needs.

2. Concept diagrams encompass the word, definition, characteristics, and examples and nonexamples of the word.

3. Word webs are effective in enriching the student's association with a word.

4. When teaching new vocabulary words, the teacher should link those words to familiar words.

5. Educators should teach the use of vocabulary resources such as the textbook glossary, dictionary, and thesaurus.

6. Vocabulary games such as dominoes, password, memory, charades, hide and seek, and scavenger hunts will assist students in learning new vocabulary words.

7. A multisensory approach is preferable with students with special needs.

8. Word banks and a card file are useful tools to assist students in learning new vocabulary words.

9

Student Response Adaptations

Journal writing was an integral part of a fifth-grade teacher's schedule. Each morning the students were to write a specific number of sentences about what had occurred the day before. The teacher was working to encourage her students to love writing as much as she did. However, journal writing presented major problems for one of her students who had a written expression problem. Joel certainly did not want to begin every day by writing in his journal because it was very difficult for him. Instead of writing, he would come in and put his head down on his desk. The teacher reminded him about the rule that he needed to write at least two sentences in his journal. The other students had to write at least four sentences—she thought she was accommodating him by reducing the number of sentences he had to write. But she quickly learned that just reducing the amount of work was not an appropriate accommodation for Joel. He would raise his head and say very loudly, "I'm not doin' this f—— journal and you can't make me." When the teacher reminded him that he had to do two sentences, he would then look at her and rip the paper up in her face. She became upset and sent him to the office, where he caused a disruption until the principal called his mother and asked her to come get him. After many days of this occurrence, the mother lost her job and was very upset with the school.

I was asked to work with the school personnel to resolve this issue. Being very sensitive to the teacher's schedule and her desire for the student to participate in the journaling activity, I asked whether she would be willing to have the student see the learning disabilities (LD) resource teacher first thing in the morning where Joel (who had good oral language skills) could dictate his sentences into a tape recorder. He and the LD teacher could then write the sentences from the tape. The student could then take his journal entry to the classroom teacher. The classroom teacher was pleased with the outcome. Later, the school purchased voice-activated software for the student.

Changing the way he could respond to the assignment made a big difference for Joel. His resource teacher also worked with him to improve his written expression skills, but in the meantime he needed a change in the response format.

This example is just one way to give an assignment and allow the student to respond in a different way. This chapter offers response adaptations that may or may not include the use of high-tech or low-tech devices. Ideas for the use of response cards are provided. There is also a section on what to do when the student won't respond—possible reasons the student may not respond and appropriate interventions that can elicit a response from the student.

USE OF TECHNOLOGY

Recently I was in a high school classroom where all of the students were expected to write a poem. The resource special educator knew that this would probably cause some passive-aggressive behavior—"I ain't writing no poem and you can't make me." The resource teacher and the general education teacher came up with a plan to motivate all the students in the class. The students were assigned a project to write a poem of a specific length and then to create a video with the poem and with music. A student who might have been a reluctant responder worked for an extended time writing the poem and creating a video. He was quite excited about the project.

In today's world, technology may be used in multiple ways to encourage student response. Students have the capacity to produce high-quality videos that show that they have learned the material. They can create a very creative project using all of the technology that is available now. It is critical, though, that the teacher keep students focused on the point of the project and tie it to what is being learned within the classroom (Jacobs, 2010).

Numerous assistive technology devices are available for students who cannot respond via paper and pencil. Examples include voice recognition systems, touch screens, adapted keyboards and switches, word processors, and electronic dictionaries, but these are just a few of the examples (Salend, 2008).

Students also can use communication boards or other communication devices to respond to questions rather than verbally or in writing (Darrow, 2007).

A student may need to provide answers with a word processor, but the student must be taught the use of that technology. If students are taught keyboarding, they can respond much quicker because the handwriting process may be very laborious for the student with fine-motor problems. The word processor also provides an additional tactile approach that may help some students to better remember the information.

For students who struggle with handwriting so much that their writing is illegible, the word processor is an excellent alternative to use until the student can be taught how to improve his or her handwriting.

Numerous types of keyboards also are available for students—those that color-code vowels, consonants, numbers, and various functions; those that have a large print keyboard for young children or for students who have difficulty with fine-motor skills; and those that have larger keys or have black on yellow letters.

An endless array of technological devices is available for the classroom. An excellent resource in most states is the Assistive Technology Network, which allows devices to be loaned and also provides training to educators and to the individuals who will be the recipients of the technology. When choosing a technological device for a student, the teacher should have an assistive technology assessment conducted by an individual who has training in that area. That individual can tell which particular device may meet the needs of the student.

Before purchasing an expensive piece of equipment, it is best to obtain it on loan to determine whether it is a match for the student and the teacher. Too many expensive pieces of equipment have been purchased and they end up in the corner of the room, either because the student did not like the device or wasn't comfortable using it, or the teacher had not received adequate training on the device and could not work with the student successfully on the technology.

LOW-TECH OPTIONS

Assistive technology that may be needed for a particular student may either be high tech or low tech. There are many low-tech devices that can be used with students with special needs. Items such as large calculators, varied pencil grips, or rulers that have a handle on them making them easier to hold are some examples. A slant board or standing at a podium rather than sitting at a desk may also be options for a student.

Some students have difficulty seeing a piece of paper on the desktop. There might be a glare on the paper on the desk. Students may be able to see the paper better if the surface was slanted. A slant board can be set at an angle on the student's desk or at a table and allows a student to see the paper better, making the writing process easier.

We make the assumption that all students respond better when they are sitting down. As mentioned in Chapter 7 on movement adaptations, some students can respond at a podium, which allows them to stand while they write their responses.

Use of a Test Booklet

When bubble sheets cause problems for students, as discussed in Chapter 12 on testing accommodations, an option may be to allow them to write their answers in a test booklet. Transferring information from a test booklet to a bubble sheet can be very problematic for some students. The student has to have adequate fine-motor skills in order to fill in the small bubbles, staying within the designated space. The student has to have a good memory to read the question, look at the possible answers, and remember the correct answer while moving her or his eyes and pencil over to the bubble sheet. The student must track adequately and make sure to match the set of bubbles to the actual question. Have you ever taken a test and got off the line and filled in the wrong bubble? It is not always easy to keep one's place.

Extra Space

Some students have a great deal of difficulty answering within a small space. If students have fine-motor difficulties, they may need additional space to write an answer. The educator can created lined paper using a word processor or can purchase larger lined paper. With older students, the teacher will need to be very careful that this does not embarrass the student in front of peers.

When the teacher is preparing worksheets or tests that require short answers, the teacher should make sure to leave enough room between questions for those students who need them. The more white space, the better for many students.

Use of a Scribe

Dictating to a scribe who then records the information is one of the most frequently allowed state testing accommodations. It is allowed by forty-three states (Bolt & Thurlow, 2004). The use of a scribe is much more common at the elementary level than it is at the secondary level. In elementary schools, 50 percent of students who use accommodations dictate to a scribe, but only 5 percent of high school students dictated their responses (Edgemon, Jablonski, & Lloyd, 2006).

To employ this accommodation appropriately and preserve its integrity, it is essential that those who will facilitate be adequately trained to ensure that they only write down exactly what is said by the student rather than interpreting what they think the student wants to say.

The Importance of Wait Time

Another strategy that is important (and is also discussed in Chapter 3) is to give a student adequate time to process information and to respond. Making statements such as "I am going to call on someone in one minute" gives all the students time to think about a response and it slows down what can otherwise turn in to a rushed lecture because the teacher is trying to cover all of the material that the students need.

Response Cards

Typically when the teacher wants students to answer questions, he or she asks the questions and students raise their hands if they know the answer. The students who don't know the answer look away from the teacher hoping the teacher doesn't call on them. The students who always know the answers always raise their hands. Other students become passive.

Research has shown that response cards reduce student disruptions in the classroom. The more students are actively engaged within the classroom, the more they are learning and therefore are not causing behavioral problems (Armendariz & Umbreit, 1999; Lambert, Cartledge, Heward, & Lo, 2006). Research also has shown that response card use increases active responses, as well as performance on weekly quizzes. Time on task was also higher with response cards opposed to hand-raising (Christle & Schuster, 2003). The following are several ways that response cards can be used in the classroom.

- Small blackboards or whiteboards offer students a place to write down their answers and hold them up for the teacher to check and for students to compare their answers with those of their peers.
- In my discussions with some teachers using Smartboards, they have mentioned that it is more motivating for students to interact on the Smartboard. It also is easier for students who have motor problems to write answers on the Smartboard rather than on the computer because it is larger for the student to use. Clickers are available so the whole classroom can respond simultaneously to a teacher's questions.
- For yes/no questions, teachers can try popsicle sticks with yes written on one and no written on another.
- For punctuation questions (e.g., which type of punctuation is required at the end of this sentence?), students can make cards with periods, question marks, or exclamation points. Or they can cut out those signs. For math problems, a teacher can read a word problem and have students hold up a card indicating which process should be used.

- Students might stand up for a yes answer, stay seated for a no answer.
- The class can play this or that. The students stand and put up a sign on each side of the room—one that says *this* and the other that says *that,* with a choice of "this" answer or "that" answer. The students move to the appropriate side of the room. There can then be a discussion about why the students thought the answer was what they thought. A variation of this is to put a large sticky note on one side of the room for yes and another one on the opposite side of the room for no. This also offers students a chance to move.

ALTERNATIVE RESPONSES

There are many ways to assess whether a student knows the material other than having that student answer a question. Some teachers utilize a tic-tac-toe, as discussed in Chapters 4 and 5. In tic-tac-toe, the students are given nine different options, each in one of the boxes. The student can complete any three that would make a tic-tac-toe (Johns & Crowley, 2007). I use tic-tac-toes as an alternative to a traditional test.

We can create a number of different types of responses for students to show us that they have learned the material. Here are just a few things a student can do.

- Create a video to depict what was learned about a topic.
- Write a poem.
- Design a game.
- Create a PowerPoint presentation about the topic.
- Draw a picture about the topic.
- Write a skit about the topic.
- Create a graphic organizer that explains the concept.
- Write a letter to the editor about the topic.
- Write a short story about the topic.

Decreasing the Quantity of Material

Teachers may want to provide some students with five spelling words per week rather than the twenty-five that the remainder of the class needs to master.

Coping With Response Resistance

Since many teachers report their frustration with students who won't respond either verbally or in writing, I have incorporated practical ideas for students who are response resistant. I have worked with such students for well over thirty years, and for many teachers these students can be the most frustrating of any group of students.

Good educators become detectives—they are always trying to figure out why students do what they do. All behavior is communication, and it is our job to figure out the reasons for student behavior. Here are some questions to ask yourself when trying to determine why a student is not responding to you either orally or in writing, as well as some possible interventions for these situations.

If the Student Is Not Responding Orally

1. Has the student been given enough time to process the information?
   A. Observe the student's processing time and allow more time for information processing if needed.
   B. Build in wait time for the student (as discussed earlier in this chapter and also in Chapter 3).
   C. Instead of requesting an oral response, let the student respond in writing using response cards.

2. Does the student understand what you are asking?
   A. Explore the vocabulary you use to determine whether the student understands what you are saying. (Chapter 8 explores vocabulary-related adaptations.)
   B. Avoid multiple-step directions. Provide one direction at a time.
   C. Limit the number of words you use in questions or in a request to respond.

3. Is the student afraid of giving the wrong answer in front of peers?
   A. Use response cards to allow the student to avoid the embarrassment.
   B. Have the students work in pairs or small groups to come up with an answer together.
   C. Set the student up for success by providing a question that you know the student can answer correctly. Then offer reinforcement for giving the correct answer, thus building up the student's confidence.

4. Is the student engaging in resistant behavior to upset you? We call such behavior passive-aggressive when the student just won't do what you want and the student knows this upsets you. The passive behavior of the student may result in frustration or aggression from you.
   A. Avoid begging and pleading. When the teacher nags, the student will dig in his or her heels even more, knowing this lack of a response upsets you.
   B. Make your request of the student twice, and then move away from the student.
   C. Be positive, be brief, and be gone. That is, ask the question in a positive manner and as briefly as possible, then move away from the student. Sometimes students just need to save face, so by

moving away you allow the student to have some time, increasing the possibility that the student will respond to your question.

D. Anytime the student does respond orally in an appropriate manner, reinforce the behavior by thanking him or her for the response. This increases the likelihood of continued positive responses because the student sees that she or he gets positive attention for giving a response rather than getting attention for negative behavior.

If the Student Is Not Responding in Writing

1. Is the student overwhelmed by the amount of work given at one time?
   A. Reduce the amount of work that is given at one time.
   B. Use the file folder cut into strips as discussed in Chapter 2.
   C. Use large print.

2. Does the student understand the directions?
   A. Review the direction words with the student ahead of time.
   B. Have the student highlight the directions ahead of time.

3. Does the student have the fine-motor skills to do the task?
   A. Consider alternative ways to provide responses, such as the use of a word processor or to give responses orally.
   B. Employ larger print and more white space to provide the response.

4. Does the student have the academic skills to do the task?

   A. Prior to giving any written assignment, use I do, we do, you do together, and you do independently, as described in Chapter 4. By using this method, the student receives plenty of modeling prior to doing the task alone.
   B. Examine the written task closely to determine whether it is appropriate for the student to do independently. If not, redo the task.
   C. Try a fading approach, wherein you provide maximum cues for the student and then reduce those cues. You may complete some of the answers, leaving only a few for the student to complete. You then can reduce the number of answers you give.

5. Is the student failing to complete the written task because the student knows that it upsets you as the teacher?
   A. Avoid begging and pleading. When the teacher nags, the student will dig in his or her heels even more, knowing this lack of a response upsets you.
   B. Request that the student begin the task. This is less overwhelming than requesting that the student complete the whole written assignment. Once the student has started a task, he or she is more

likely to stick with it. The teacher should then offer reinforcement to the student for beginning the task.

C. Provide a choice of how the student can respond. The student can do the assignment in a green pen or a red pen, can do any three rows of math problems, can do the odd or even numbered problems.

D. Make the request twice that you want the student to start the written assignment, and then move away from the student.

E. Be positive, be brief, and be gone. That is, ask the question in a positive manner and as briefly as possible, then move away from the student. Sometimes students just need to save face, so by moving away you allow the student to have some time, increasing the possibility that the student will do the worksheet.

F. Avoid the use of questions. Asking "Would you like to do this worksheet?" tells the student that he or she has a choice, which is not the case in this situation. Instead of asking a question, state, "I need you to start on this assignment." And state specifically what you want the student to do on the written assignment.

Summary: Just 3×5 It

1. Many technological devices allow for student responses. An excellent resource is the Assistive Technology Network, available in most states.

2. When selecting a technological device, there should be an assistive technology assessment to determine the specific needs of the student.

3. One response accommodation is the use of a scribe.

4. Response cards can reduce behavioral problems in the classroom. Types of response cards range from no tech to high tech.

5. Alternative responses may include tic-tac-toe, in which students choose the type of response they will give.

6. The educator may consider reducing how much is required from a student in a response.

7. When students are response resistant, it is critical to look at the possible reason for the resistance.

8. A number of possible interventions can be used when the teacher determines the reason for response resistance.

10

Timing/Scheduling Adaptations

When teachers hear about timing adaptations, they automatically think of extended timelines because that is one of the most frequently utilized adaptations, especially for testing. Educators tend to think that giving the student more time will assist all of them. Extended timelines is a needed accommodation for many students who require additional time because it takes them longer to read the information or they have a delayed processing time when reading or listening to directions.

Extended timelines are needed also for those students who have a high level of anxiety and become very stressed under time pressure. They do not do well on timed tests because their anxiety interferes with the task.

However, there is another side to the issue of extended timelines. In the introductory chapter, I discussed the importance of teaching the child how to use an accommodation and why we can't just accommodate students without also providing them with the specialized instruction that is needed. Extended timelines is a good example. If we provide extended timelines to a student who does not know how to manage time effectively, this accommodation may be a hindrance instead of a help. For example, if the student is told that he has twice as much time to complete a task, he may choose to waste a lot of the time because he thinks he has a lot more of it, but he still ends up not completing the task because he didn't know how to manage his time.

This chapter therefore focuses on strategies for teaching children how to manage their time so that they can benefit from extended timelines.

We live in a society that is built on time schedules. I once heard someone say that if you have a disability that affects your ability to manage your own time, it can be debilitating to you. I thought long and hard about that statement and realized how true it is. Our entire society is focused on time. We have to be at work at a certain time—if we don't show up on time for a few days, we will lose our job. If we are supposed to meet our friends for dinner and fail to show up on time, our friends begin to lose patience with us and will not invite us to dinner again, and we may lose those individuals as friends. If we have a doctor's appointment and don't show up on time, we may be billed for the appointment anyway for being a no-show. In school, if we don't get to class on time, we may fail the class. All of these situations cause us to pause and realize the importance of teaching our children how to manage their own time.

Because of our society's focus on time, we live in a rushed society. People want to get things quickly. Many people eat fast food. We want our Internet access to be high speed. We don't want to wait in lines and we want easy solutions to our problems. Everyone tries to multitask to get lots of things done within a twenty-four hour period. The new generation of children is being called the *mobile generation* because they will live in a world where they multitask with electronic devices to get things done.

Teachers don't always pause and take the time to listen to students because they are in such a hurry. Teachers feel stressed and their students quickly pick up on that stress and become stressed as well. We want our students to complete their assignments quickly, but some students just can't do it. They may exhibit behavior problems because of their frustration and stress. Some of our children simply can't keep up with all we expect them to do. While we all thought that technology was going to make our lives easier, we seem to be expected to do even more in less time.

In this country, we don't always have the tolerance for other cultures that don't rush around as much as we do. Other cultures may take a siesta in the afternoon—we can't understand how anyone can have the time to take time off in the middle of the day. When we work with children from different places, we must consider their culture and the fact that they value a more leisurely pace than we do.

THE IMPORTANCE OF KNOWING STUDENTS' PROCESSING TIME

Some children need more time to hear what the teacher is saying to them, process what is being said, and provide an appropriate response. Students with learning disabilities have difficulty processing information either aurally or in writing. We can't work successfully with children in our classrooms without knowing their processing time.

I remember working with Dewayne, a seventeen-year-old with cognitive disabilities. Teachers were complaining that he wouldn't do what they asked of him. Instead Dewayne would just stand or sit and stare at the teacher, who would become very aggravated with him, thinking that he was just being obnoxious and refusing to comply. When I started working with Dewayne, I had a feeling there was more going on with Dewayne. It didn't appear that he was being obnoxious; it just seemed that he needed more time. Through observations, I learned that it took ninety-five seconds for Dewayne to respond when given a request because it took him that long to process the information and provide a response. Many teachers may lack the patience to wait that long, but Dewayne's disability meant he needed more time to process information.

How do we learn more about a student's processing time? It is important to observe the student closely to gather this information. If we aren't sure about how long it takes our students to process information, we may want to ask someone else to observe the student. We also will want to review previous evaluations and reports from other teachers to determine relevant information about the student's processing time.

Desensitizing Children to Timed Tasks and Tests

Our children should be slowly desensitized to time demands. In life there will be a lot of time demands on them, so they need to know how to work within a time frame. The teacher can accommodate these students by teaching them how to complete timed tests gradually. A student can be given a timed test involving a task that the student likes and can do easily. The teacher can start by giving the student the task and offering the student more time than she or he believes it will take the student to complete it. When the student completes the task, the teacher should offer positive reinforcement, attributing the student's success to his or her effort. The student can even chart his or her progress for getting the task done within the given time frame. During the next session, the teacher can give the child a little less time, and when the student completes the task, the teacher again should provide reinforcement. The amount of time the student has to do a task continues to be gradually decreased. The student continues to chart the progress so she or he sees that progress is being made. Once the student has been desensitized to the timed tasks, more difficult tasks may be introduced.

CHANGING THE SETTING WHEN A STUDENT NEEDS EXTENDED TIMELINES

We all may have experienced the anxiety of taking a test within a large group and someone or several people completed the test before we did.

We then worried that everyone else would complete the test before we did and that they were doing better because they finished earlier. Talk about feeling time pressure.

Serious consideration should be given to providing a separate room for any students who need extended timelines so that they do not feel pressured to rush to get the test or the assignment done when everyone else does. This may not always be possible, but it certainly can reduce the stress on the student who needs an extended timeline.

USING VISUAL TIMERS

Many years ago we used kitchen timers for a variety of activities in the classroom. The teacher might play the timer game with the students; that is, the timer would be set at random times and when it rang whoever was on task got some type of reward. This game is still very popular, though it has to be used cautiously with students who are very sensitive to noise.

Some students with autism may fixate on when the timer will go off, becoming very upset for an extended period from the worry about when the timer will go off. Also, timers that make noise may be very bothersome to some students. Therefore, some timers are now visual. The teacher states that students have fifteen minutes to complete a task and sets the visual timer, which shows red for the fifteen minutes. The red color then moves according to how much time is left, and when the time is up no red shows.

Visual timers are very effective for students, and not just those with autism. For students who do not have a sense of time—they don't know what fifteen minutes looks like—these timers are very effective. I have found that they work with all ages of students because they lend structure to the student's day. Now, the same concept has been used to develop an individual student watch that provides the red cues for how much time remains before the next activity. The student wears the watch and is told how much time is allowed to complete a task. The student can then set the watch. As with the timer, the red will show, and when the red is gone, the time is up.

TEACHING STUDENTS TO MEET DEADLINES

We live in a world full of deadlines. We have to get reports done by a certain time. We have to file information by a certain date. We have to pay our bills on time. But meeting deadlines may be very difficult for students with special needs. They may think they have plenty of time to do an assignment so they don't work on it until it is close to the due date. They may be unable to manage their time and put the assignment off until it is almost due, only to have life get in the way of completing the assignment—they get sick, they lose their appointment book, or something else becomes a greater priority.

Other students can keep up with assignments for a time but then they get overwhelmed and shut down. I have worked with so many students who become overwhelmed, shut down, and then get nothing done and fail classes because they didn't complete their assignments.

The teacher must teach students how to complete things before deadline and not wait until the last minute. Here are a few techniques I have used successfully.

- The teacher can provide bonus points to students who complete the assignment ahead of schedule—perhaps one week or two days before the deadline, whatever seems reasonable. The teacher should point out to the students how much they reduce their stress and how much better they feel when they get something done ahead of schedule.
- The teacher can break the assignment down into small parts so that students don't get overwhelmed. For example, if the teacher has assigned a research paper in a high school class, the teacher can break down the assignment with due dates for each step. Perhaps one chapter is due by a certain date, another is due by a later date, another is due by a third date, and the remainder of the paper is due by the deadline. This teaches students the importance of breaking down a large task into small parts.
- The teacher can work with the students to write down the specific due dates of each assignment in their appointment book so they remember when an assignment is due. (See the section on appointment books later in this chapter.)

OFFERING TIME-ESTIMATION SHEETS

It may be difficult for some students to determine how long it will take them to do a specific assignment. From an early age, students need to learn to estimate how long a task will take. The teacher can provide time-estimation sheets with each assignment. The student has to write down an estimate of how long it will take to complete the assignment. Once the assignment is completed, the student writes down how long it actually took to complete the assignment. Over time, students' estimates become more accurate as they learn how to better estimate time.

PLAYING BEAT THE CLOCK

This is a fun activity to do with students who are passive-aggressive when they put their heads down on their desk and refuse to do what is expected of them. I used this effectively with a student who was very bright but had significant behavioral problems. When given an assignment to complete, he would put his head down on the desk and say, "I'm not doing this." The tasks were clearly ones that he could do independently. I learned to say to him, "Andrew, I bet that assignment will take you five minutes to do." Then I set the timer. Andrew always got it done ahead of time because he wanted to prove me wrong.

TEACHING STUDENTS TO SCHEDULE THEMSELVES

The teacher must teach students the importance of managing their own time. Students have to identify the time wasters that get in their way of accomplishing what is important. Teachers can help students recognize and write down their time wasters, and then to develop a plan to reduce them. Students should be taught to make daily lists of what they hope to accomplish. As they accomplish those tasks, they cross the item off the list.

Keeping an Appointment or Agenda Book

A critical demand faced by middle and high school students is the need to organize, keep track of, and complete the assignments within a specific time frame. To do that, students need to be taught to use either an electronic or a written appointment or agenda book. Such an appointment book is important for older students because they are moving from teacher to teacher and in many cases, with no adult to check in with them at the end of the day to make sure that they have all their assignments written down and know what they need to do.

If students don't complete their assignments, they face a strong likelihood that they will not pass their classes. Students must be able to listen when the teacher gives the assignment, they have to know when the assignment is due, and they must know what books they need to take home to do the assignments. Students with special needs who have organizational problems have a great deal of difficulty with this. They may forget to write down the assignment or they can't read what they have written down. A good mnemonic—TRICK BAG—was created by Scott and Compton (2007) and can assist students with this task. The mnemonic is as follows:

T—Take out agenda book.

R—Record the assignment.

I—Insert the important details.

C—Circle materials that are needed.

K—Keep materials in a homework folder.

B—Be sure you can read it.

A—Ask a partner to check it.

G—Go put it in your backpack.

Keeping a Schedule

Some students with special needs have difficulty keeping a schedule of what they need to do and when they need to do it. Many electronic and manual devices are available to create a schedule for the day, week, or month. Teachers model the use of schedules when they post what is going to happen and when. Teachers also prepare students for changes in the schedule. Some students need a picture schedule—not just students who can't read, but other students may need a visual reminder as a prompt to better understand what needs to be done.

Some teachers prepare a left-right schedule and others prepare a top-to-bottom schedule. Some then cross off the activities as they are completed so the students see what they have accomplished. Students also have preferences for types of schedules—left to right or top to bottom and it is critical that the teacher learn what works best for each student. If a student is not responding to a schedule, that format may not be the preference of the student.

One of my favorite ways to create the schedule in classes for older students is to write the specific activities planned for the period on sticky notes that are the size of a half sheet of paper. I post them on the board, left to right in the front of the room. When one activity is completed, I pull the sticky note off the board, until all activities have been completed. I learned that in some of my classes, I had students who preferred a top-to-bottom schedule. In those cases, I did both schedules. Interestingly, there have been times when I have forgotten to pull a sticky note off the board when we finish an activity and a student will go up and do so. By using sticky notes, I am showing students that they can make reminders to themselves about tasks they need to do, and when they complete the task they can destroy the sticky note.

Students should be taught to keep lists and a schedule in order to keep themselves focused on what they need to do during the day.

Making Transitions

It can be difficult for students with special needs to transition from one activity to another. Many of us don't like to change, and once we start on a task we want to stick with it until we complete it. Within the classroom and in today's society, we have to learn to make transitions. Teachers move from one activity to another activity. Some children with special needs may perseverate—they keep doing the same thing over and over again and they don't want to stop. I have found that children with autism often become accustomed to one activity—especially if it was a preferred activity—and do not want to stop.

Here are some ways to help children to make transitions.

- Provide a statement such as "We have three more minutes before we move into our math activity."
- Use a visual timer to show how many minutes are left in an activity.
- Reinforce those students who begin to put items away before it is time to start the next activity. "I appreciate the way that Jan is getting ready for our next lesson."
- Dim the lights when it is time for one activity to be completed and another to begin.
- Play music to signify the end of an activity.

Summary: Just 3×5 It

1. Extended timelines are a common accommodation for a student, but there are cautions with this accommodation, such as making sure the student can effectively make use of the extension.

2. Teaching students to manage their own time is an important life skill.

3. Teaching students how to estimate time needed to complete an assignment is a necessary classroom skill.

4. Beat the clock is one adaptation that can be used for passive-aggressive students.

5. Educators must learn each student's processing time.

6. The availability of visual timers is important for each classroom.

7. Educators should recognize students who complete assigned tasks prior to a deadline.

8. Students should be exposed to different ways to maintain a schedule in order to determine what type of schedule works best for them.

11

Note-Taking
Adaptations

Creating Swiss cheese notes describes how some students write down what has been said in class. When the student is taking notes, the teacher continues to talk, saying things that are important. But the student is concentrating so much on the writing that he or she misses some important points. Consequently students' notes have holes, thus the notes look like Swiss cheese.

The process of taking notes is difficult for students with special needs because it involves so many skills: listening to what is being said, processing the information, conducting the motor skills involved in writing, remembering what was said while writing it down, understanding the vocabulary and concepts being discussed, blocking out extraneous stimuli, picking out what is important, abbreviating key terms, and then reviewing the notes and figuring out what was written down. Wow, is it any wonder our students with special needs have difficulty with note taking? How many times have we written a simple note to ourselves and later wondered what we meant by it? Just yesterday I wrote myself a note and later couldn't read my own handwriting.

This chapter focuses on adaptations that the teacher can make in facilitating the note-taking process for students.

TOOLS TO ASSIST IN NOTE TAKING

Note Takers

One of the most frequently used adaptations for note taking is the use of a note taker, another student who is proficient in taking notes actually does so for the student who struggles with the process. If this is done, it is a good idea to purchase carbon note paper. Such paper allows the student who takes the notes to immediately give them to the person who needs them. Too often, the student takes the notes, has to give the notes to the teacher to make a copy of them, and then the teacher has to give the notes back to both students. In today's rushed society, this takes time from the teacher. While carbon note paper may cost more, it is well worth the cost.

Another option is to have the note taker work with a laptop computer so that immediately after class the notes can be e-mailed to the student who needs them.

A major caution should be considered when using a note taker: it encourages passive learning on the part of the student with special needs. If someone else is taking the notes for the student, the student does not accept responsibility for paying attention to what is being said in class. As a result, the student with special needs may zone out during the lesson. It is therefore important that while the student has a note taker, the student also should be taught how to take notes, beginning with a simplified process. The teacher may want to assign the student to write two key points that were addressed within the lecture, or the teacher may want to provide a graphic organizer in which the student has to complete three or four points. That way the student will then have the opportunity to review the note taker's notes and at the same time has some responsibility for actually taking notes.

The teacher may want to give the student a framed outline of the lecture in which the student only has to complete two or three fill-in blanks. Slowly then, the teacher can increase the amount of information that the student must record.

Guided Notes

Guided note taking provides an alternative method to traditional note taking and increases students' engagement with the process. When a student has a note taker or is just given notes in some format, the student is not engaged. A recent meta-analytic review of guided notes showed the process of using them to be an effective one (Konrad, Joseph, & Eveleigh, 2009). Guided notes provide the student with a skeleton outline that lists the main points of the lecture and also provide spaces for the students to complete as the teacher expounds on each main idea. Students are provided with the guided notes prior to the teacher's lecture and are asked to complete the outline during the lecture. Such an outline provides the main ideas for the student (Weishaar & Boyle, 1999). After the lecture, the teacher might want to give a fun quiz about the content of the guided notes to see how many of the main points the student could provide. The teacher may want the students to turn in the notes at the end of the lecture period, especially when the students are learning how to use this process. That way the teacher can check on whether the student has grasped the key concepts.

Strategic Note Taking

Another note-taking method that promotes active student engagement is strategic note taking. In this method, the teacher provides a note-taking form that contains written cues to help the students use metacognitive skills during lectures. Weishaar and Boyle (1999) outline the steps in this process. First the student is asked to identify the lecture topic and then to relate the topic to their own knowledge. Then the students are asked to cluster together three to seven major points with details from the lecture as the lecture is being presented. They are again at the end of the page asked to summarize information given during the lecture. The last step is a quick review of the lecture after it has ended. Weishaar and Boyle found this method to be more effective for students with mild disabilities than traditional note taking.

Column Format for Notes

There are a number of variations when using a column format for notes. One suggested format would be three columns, with one being for basic ideas, the second being for background information, and the third being for questions the student might have (Weishaar & Boyle, 1999).

Graphic Organizers

We are all familiar with the use of graphic organizers and many examples are readily available to us. The advantages of such organizers are many. They are a visual depiction of what is going to be said or what was said. The teacher can begin the lecture with a graphic organizer so that the students get the big picture of what will be discussed. The teacher can also end the lecture with a graphic organizer as a review of what has been said. Another option is for the student to create his or her own graphic organizer to help him or her as an aid to remembering key information. Graphic organizers increase retention for students, they identify misconceptions and clarify knowledge, and they can encourage creativity for students (Grant, 2009).

Inspiration is a software tool that can be used to create graphic organizers. Grant (2009) encourages the use of Inspiration because a linear outline is automatically created with the graphic organizer diagram view. As a result, the teacher or the student creates a creative diagram view and also sees a linear outline that is a logical view and vice versa. This taps into the talents of both types of students—those who are more creative and those who are more logical. I have never had a preference for graphic organizers because I tend to be a very logical individual, yet Inspiration allows me to see both the diagram and a linear outline at the same time.

Abbreviations

It seems to be easier now to teach the concept of using abbreviations with the real world of text messaging. Everyone is abbreviating. A colleague reported that he even got a paper from a student that had a few of the text messaging abbreviations.

When abbreviations are used in the subject of the lecture, those abbreviations, along with the vocabulary, should be taught ahead of time so students are familiar with the abbreviations prior to beginning to take notes. As an example, if the lecture involves the Underground Railroad, the abbreviations for the states involved is helpful to the student.

Verbal Cues

When the teacher is making an important point that she or he wants to make sure the student remembers, the teacher should stop and state, "This is an important point." For interest purposes, the teacher should vary voice inflections. The voice can be raised slightly to make a critical point. The critical points can be repeated. The key points can be provided at the beginning of the lecture and again at the end of the lecture. Or the teacher can use some fun attention getting devices when about to give a key point, such as saying, "Hear ye, hear ye." Sound effects can also be employed prior to making a key point. The teacher also can mention the key point and then have all students repeat the key point in unison.

An Advanced Copy of the Notes

I was participating in an Individualized Education Program (IEP) for a high school student some time ago and the parent was an active participant who wanted to help her son in his social studies class. He was easily distracted in class and came home with very few notes. She would try to help him, but it was difficult to review the information with him because he had such sketchy notes. She asked the high school teacher whether he would be willing to let her have a copy of his notes the night before the lecture. The high school teacher was very accommodating and willing to do so. The parent could review the information with her son the night before he listened to the class lecture. Then when he went into the lecture period, he was more attentive because he was familiar with the information and felt like he knew something already.

Breaks to Review Notes

Whatever method of note taking is chosen, it is advisable for the teacher to stop frequently during the lecture and ask that students, either with a partner or in a small group, review their notes so that they have an opportunity to process the information and also to compare and contrast the notes that they took with their fellow students.

Teacher Review of Notes

If the teacher has the time after class or has the help of an assistant, the teacher may want to review the student's notes, particularly before the student takes the notes home to study for a test.

MAKING THE MOTOR PROCESS OF TAKING NOTES AS EASY AS POSSIBLE FOR THE STUDENT

Students with significant fine-motor problems may have trouble staying within the lines, moving from left to right, keeping their place on their paper, or controlling their pencil. These problems will cause the student to have difficulty taking notes, even if he or she can process the information that the teacher provides. If you are concentrating so hard on staying within the lines or controlling your pencil, you will lose sight of what the teacher says.

Here are some strategies the teacher can use to assist the student who has motor problems.

- Supply paper with widely spaced lines. The student may need extra space within which to write, so the teacher can use the computer to make note paper that has more space.
- Provide arrows or other visual cues to help the student move from left to right. The teacher may want to put an arrow or some other sign where the student should begin on the piece of paper.

- Provide different pencils or pens, or pencil grips. The teacher may want to provide the student with a larger pencil or pen. Now there are also pens shaped like scissors and that are more ergonomically correct. These may work for some students. Pencil grips come in a variety of shapes and textures, so the teacher will want to give the student the opportunity to experiment with what will work best for the student.
- For students who struggle with writing, use a word processor when appropriate. An added benefit for the student, besides the assistance with the motor process, is that some students are more likely to remember the information because they have had the additional tactile sense to assist them in remembering the material. Some of us use a word processor so much now that we realize how laborious and sometimes tiring it is to have to write our notes by hand. Again, you as the teacher will have to determine whether the student can use a regular size keyboard or needs a large keyboard. Talking word processors are also now available for students.

MAKING THE AUDITORY PROCESS OF TAKING NOTES AS EASY AS POSSIBLE FOR THE STUDENT

Taking notes requires that the student attend to what the teacher says, process the information, remember what has just been said, and then translate that to the fine-motor skills necessary to write down or to type the material.

For students who have difficulty processing information that they hear, the teacher will need to make adaptations to ensure that the student understands. The following are some adaptations that the teacher can make to facilitate the processing of auditory information.

- Provide an advance organizer with the key points that will be included in the lecture.
- Plan to repeat key points.
- After making a key point, stop for a short time to give the students the chance to record the information. The teacher might want to lecture for a few minutes and then model how to take notes. The teacher could lecture for three to five minutes and then stop and using a think-aloud could say, "Let me review what I think are the most important points." The teacher then writes down the two or three key points on a projector or the Smartboard. The teacher thus demonstrates how he or she thinks aloud to answer questions and think about the key points.

- Combine visual information with auditory information and provide access to the visual information. The teacher can give the lecture using a PowerPoint and also can provide the students a copy of the PowerPoint presentation done with space for notes. However, the teacher should consider the following points when using a PowerPoint presentation.

    o Avoid using abbreviations that have not been specifically taught to the students.

    o Avoid too many words per slide.

    o Avoid putting too many bells and whistles in the slide presentation. I remember well an inservice I was doing for administrators. I had decided to make a very fancy presentation and built in sounds for each of the sections of the slides. Several administrators commented that it was just too distracting for them—they were more focused on the sounds and had difficulty attending to the meat of the presentation. This will be true of some of our students as well.

    o Try to use sentences opposed to phrases. One of the problems with bulleted points in the presentations that we prepare is that students begin to get used to phrases and are not exposed to enough sentence structure.

- Some type of amplification system might make it easier for some students to attend.

NOTE-TAKING STRATEGIES

A number of note-taking strategies are appropriate for students. These strategies need to be taught to the student systematically, one step at a time and with a great deal of opportunity for students to practice.

CALL UP

This strategy, developed by Czarnecki, Rosko, and Fine (1998), was designed for students to use while taking notes in class.

C—Copy from the board or projector.

A—Add details.

L—Listen to the question that the teacher asks and that students ask, and write it down if it helps understanding. Put a *Q* in front of the question.

L—Listen and write the answer.

U—Utilize the text. When you are at home, use the textbook to review and better understand information. Review the main ideas in the textbook.

P—Put ideas in your own words.

A NOTES

Another strategy to teach students to use for reviewing notes and revising after the classroom presentation is "A-Notes" (Czarnecki, Rosko, & Fine, 1998).

A—Ask yourself if you have the date and topic notes.

N—Name the main ideas and details.

O—Observe the ideas also in the text.

T—Try noting in the margin using the SAND substrategy.

    S—Star the important ideas.

    A—Arrange arrows to connect ideas.

    N—Number key points in order.

    D—Devise abbreviations and write them down next to the item.

E—Examine to check for omissions or unclear ideas.

S—Summarize key points.

Experimenting With Different Methods of Taking Notes

Chapter 1 discusses the importance of considering the student's preferences when determining accommodations. When it comes to note taking, what works for one student may not work for another. Teachers should expose their students to a variety of note-taking strategies so that students can find what will work best for them. A couple of alternative ways for taking notes follow. These techniques can be used together with any of the other methods described in this chapter. For example, the student may have used guided notes and then rewrites the guided notes in one of the following formats.

Notes in a Bag

I have found that some students with ADHD prefer to take notes on 3×5 index cards so that when they go home they can pace as they study the note cards. I began suggesting this to some students after I was told by a friend with ADHD that this was the way that she got through graduate school. She took her notes on 3×5 cards and then brought them home to pace back and forth while she studied the notes.

If you are going to implement this with a student, it is important that you provide the student with a plastic or paper bag in which to keep the notes contained. Otherwise the index cards will end up all over the place, and some will probably be lost. If bags are used, the student may mark on the outside of the bag the subject to which the notes pertain.

Puzzles

As mentioned in Chapter 7, this is a fun way to take notes, and some students with ADHD like to take notes in this manner because they can physically manipulate the information. The teacher provides the student with a sheet of paper that is marked into puzzle pieces. The number of puzzle pieces will vary depending on the age of the student. Even with older students, I like to limit the number of puzzle pieces to no more than twenty. The student puts one key concept on each piece of the puzzle. Again, the student can transfer the information from guided notes or strategic notes or column notes. Another option is for the student to take notes directly onto the puzzle pieces. The student then cuts the piece of paper into the puzzle pieces and puts the pieces in a bag. To study, the student can put the puzzle pieces back together. This gives the student the opportunity to physically manipulate the material.

CAUTIONS ON WHERE TO KEEP NOTES

Spiral Bound Notebooks

One will have to be very careful when using spiral bound notebooks with left-handed students, unless the student has a left-handed notebook. The spirals on a regular notebook will be a barrier for a left-handed student, making it difficult to write information down. The student may then get frustrated and give up.

Three-Ring Binders

Some students prefer to keep their notes in a three-ring binder and put everything for one class in one notebook. Others do not like to use a three-ring binder because they find them awkward or they don't want to take the time to punch the papers and put them in the binder (I am one of those individuals).

Be cautious too of using three-ring binders for students who are left-handed, unless you purchase one specifically designed for a left-handed student. Otherwise, the rings get in the way of the student who writes with the left hand.

File Folders

Some students prefer to organize their notes into file folders according to the subject. For students with ADHD who prefer this method, it is recommended that file pockets be used rather than open file folders because it is too easy for the papers to fall out of a standard file folder.

TEACHING STUDENTS WHAT TO DO WITH THE NOTES THEY'VE TAKEN

How many students do we know who take notes and then don't study them? Or don't open them until it is time to study for a test—by then they don't remember what they meant when they wrote something down. Some students can't read their own writing. It is important for teachers to devote a short amount of time before each class period ends for students to review their notes and ask any questions that they may have. Students must be taught to review their notes as soon as possible after taking them; otherwise students forget what they meant when they wrote down the concepts. Such a review gives them time to ask the teacher or another student what was meant by a certain point. The teacher should always provide a brief review of what was taught during the lecture. The teacher can provide the three or four key points covered during the lecture. That way the student hears the most important information again.

Spending Time Reflecting Before the End of the Period

I like to do an activity before the end of the period in which the students draw a piece of paper out of a hat or jar. Each piece of paper has a different reflective question on it.

- What is the most important point you learned today?
- What is something you heard today that you are likely to never forget?
- What is something you learned today with which you don't agree?
- What was the least important piece of information you learned?

Summary: Just 3×5 It

1. If the student has a note taker, it is important that the student get the notes immediately after the lecture, either electronically or through the use of carbon paper.

2. Guided notes and strategic note taking are two effective strategies that engage students in the process.

3. Students can create graphic organizers to assist them in remembering key points.

4. It is critical that students learn abbreviations in order to take notes.

5. The educator should provide prompts for students during lectures and should stop periodically so students can review notes.

6. The educator must facilitate the motor process and the auditory process of taking notes.

7. Effective note-taking strategies include CALL UP and A-NOTES.

8. Educators should expose students to different methods of taking notes, as well as where to keep notes, so that each student learns what works best for him or her.

12

Testing Adaptations

Today's teachers are faced with the tremendous stress of preparing students for statewide testing, and often teachers are judged based on how well their students do on the test, even when teachers cannot control many of the variables that may be responsible for how well the student does.

The IEP team or the Section 504 team, who work together to develop a plan about the specific individualized needs of the student, has a serious responsibility in determining needed testing accommodations for the student. They must determine the appropriate accommodations that don't jeopardize the integrity of the test, yet meet the needs of the student. Throughout this book, you have been provided with a whole array of accommodations that can be made within the classroom setting. Many of those accommodations can be applied within the test-taking environment.

Whatever accommodations are selected by the team, they should be ones that are used in instruction too. If it is determined that the child may use a calculator during certain portions of the math test, then the calculator also should be used as an accommodation within the instructional process. The student has to be familiar and comfortable with the accommodation and has to have been taught how to use it. Otherwise, the accommodation may not be effective for the student.

Testing accommodations require careful planning in advance, monitoring during the test, and planning after the test for needed changes. In advance, the IEP or Section 504 team outlines the critical accommodations that the student needs within instruction and in assessment. The teacher then must work with the student within instruction to determine which accommodations work and which do not. The teacher must work closely to build the student's awareness of what is effective and what is not effective.

During the testing, it is critical that someone observe how the student is actually using the accommodation and whether it appears to be effective for the student. That information should be written down so that it can be considered when decisions are being made for the next round of tests. As an example, extended timelines may have been recommended for a student, but when the student takes the test the teacher observes that the student completes the test before some of the other students. This information should be shared with the IEP or Section 504 team so that the accommodation may be reconsidered for future testing.

TRAINING OF INDIVIDUALS WHO ADMINISTER TESTING ACCOMMODATIONS

It is necessary for the individuals who will be involved in providing the testing accommodations to receive training on how to do so. One might think that it is very easy for someone to read the test to a student. However, it is very difficult to remain objective in the process.

The person administering the test should not be giving the student the answers. That individual is to remain very objective and only provide the amount of assistance needed, not to give students prompts that might help them to answer the test question.

Picture this scenario: The teacher really wants the student to do well on the test. The teacher reads the question and the four possible answers, but when the teacher gets to the correct answer, her voice inflection rises. She doesn't even realize she has done this, but in fact she has given the student a strong signal about the correct answer.

Here's another scenario: As the teacher monitors the test, he moves around the room, giving emotional support. He sees a student struggling with a question and goes over to check how the student is doing. The student begins to fill in a square but is hesitant. The teacher says, "great," thereby prompting the student about the right answer.

INPUT AND OUTPUT

When determining the testing accommodations during the IEP or Section 504 process, the team will need to determine what type of input the student will need to take the test—that is, how will the student take in the information on the test? Will the test need to be read aloud, will it be presented in large print, will the student need an interpreter?

The output determines how the student will demonstrate his or her answers. Will the student be able to dictate answers to an instructor, will the student be able to type responses, can the student answer on the test sheet rather than on the infamous bubble sheets?

UNIVERSAL DESIGN IN TESTING

The Individuals with Disabilities Education Act (IDEA) of 2004 allows for the use of universal design in statewide testing. Universal design is an exciting concept that allows text to be digitized so that the student can use a computer, and the software is available that includes the accommodation. For example, the test is digitized and the software provides a voice that reads the test to the student. This better maintains the integrity of the test because a real person who is reading a test to the student may unknowingly clue the student the correct answers by voice inflection. Software also allows key words to be highlighted, such as direction words. More on universal design can be found at the Center for Applied Special Technology website (http://www.cast.org/).

Universal design allows the student to view information in a variety of formats that enable him or her to access the curriculum and the test. It allows students to review the information on the test as many times as possible.

THINKING OUT OF THE BOX
ON TEST ACCOMMODATIONS

You may be wondering what this section is about. Simply put, we shouldn't quickly assume that certain accommodations are only useful for certain populations of students with disabilities. As an example, large print material is a common accommodation for a student who is visually impaired. Yet, it also may be very appropriate for a student with a learning disability who has visual perception problems and has difficulty with smaller print. Large print materials also may be appropriate for a student who has emotional or behavioral disorders because the student becomes very frustrated with small print and feels more comfortable with larger print. The student may be overwhelmed by small print yet can cope with larger print on the page.

Children who are hard of hearing may require sound amplification when teachers are reading the directions for a test. This accommodation also may be appropriate for a student who has attention problems and the amplification may help her or him to better focus. It may be appropriate for the student with a learning disability or the student with autism who has difficulty blocking out extraneous sounds during that time.

Chapter 5 on behavioral adaptations discussed the importance of giving students power and control by giving them choices. We can allow the student to have a choice about the particular pencil to use. Now a very motivating pencil for some students is one that has a particular smell. Students from kindergarten through high school seem to like pencils that smell like root beer, peppermint, or sugar cookie.

We also might want to give the student a choice of where in a room to take the test. A student may prefer to work at a table rather than at a desk. If several students want to work at a table, it will be important to use partitions on the table so that the students cannot see the work of the others at the table.

We seem to assume that students have to take the test in a specific order when, for some students, the order of the test administration may need to be changed. If the math is usually administered before the reading and the student has a great deal of difficulty in math, the student feels defeated before even beginning because the student expects to do poorly on the math. If the student's strength is in reading, consideration should be given to completing the reading test first so the student meets with success.

DEALING WITH THE ANXIETY OF TESTS

One of the worst cases of test anxiety that I had ever seen was a young lady who was so stressed out over a test that she misspelled her own name. Learning is indeed an emotional issue, and this student was so emotionally stressed over the test that she forgot a simple skill that clearly she knew when she was in a nonthreatening environment. How many of us have demonstrated that we know the answer to a question but then when we get into the test we forget the information? Very few people like to take tests, so testing evokes a high level of anxiety. Research has shown that some of the reactions that are associated with worry, such as lack of concentration and distractions to attention, can contribute to decreases in scores on cognitive intellectual tasks (Carter et al., 2005; Liebert & Morris, 1967).

We must teach the child how to deal with the anxiety that typically comes from taking the test. The remainder of this section deals with practical ideas about how to assist our children in overcoming anxiety.

Building Positive Affect

A number of studies were conducted by Tanis Bryan and her colleagues (Bryan & Bryan, 1991; Bryan, Sullivan-Burstein, & Mathur, 1998; Yasutake & Bryan, 1996) on self-induced positive affect on learning and performance of students with learning disabilities. A positive affect was self-induced by having students close their eyes and think of something positive for forty-five seconds (Bryan, Sullivan-Burstein, & Mathur, 1998).

In studies of students with learning disabilities from primary grades through high school, the students who could do this on a variety of tasks—including vocabulary, speed in math problems, and coding—increased their achievement in those tasks.

Prior to administering a test, I have my students close their eyes for forty-five seconds and think of something that makes them happy. This puts the students in a more positive frame of mind and assists them in tackling the test. It is an easy intervention for teachers to employ.

Positive Self Talk

We have all heard students make negative statements about themselves and we, at some time, make negative statements about ourselves: I'm not any good at math, I just can't do this, I have no talent in art, or I'm having a bad day. When individuals say such things over and over they begin to believe them and it impacts how they do on a task. If I say, "I'm having a bad day," it impacts my performance that day because I begin to build every problem I face out of proportion.

On the other hand, if we use positive statements to ourselves, we believe them. If I am driving on ice, I talk to myself and say, "I can do this; I'm a good driver." I begin to internalize this belief and can face the challenge of driving on ice.

Our students have to be taught directly to make positive statements about themselves. We need to reinforce them when we hear them saying statements like "Math is my strong subject," or "I'm a good reader." Many older students with special needs will come into the classroom with such statements as "I hate English." This certainly does impact how they will do in English. We, as educators, then need to look for what the student does well and say, "See you wrote some very creative statements," or "I am impressed with your use of correct grammar." The teacher looks for positive things to say to students so that they recognize their strengths and can engage in positive self talk.

The teacher must be the role model for the student and should make positive statements about himself or herself so that students can see that positive self talk is okay. Here are three activities that I have used with students at varying ages.

1. **Recognizing their own strengths.** I do an activity with students in which they are given a picture of a tree with its roots. On each root they have to write positive statements about themselves.

2. **Reinforcing positive statements and catching negative thoughts.** I like to work with students to make positive statements about themselves. I conduct lessons on positive self talk and offer examples of it. I then reinforce students when I hear them make such statements. When they make a negative statement about themselves, they have to mark that they did so on a piece of paper. Each day they make no negative statements, they receive some type of positive recognition.

3. **Congratulating their peers.** At the end of the day, each student is given enough sheets of paper for each student in the class. This works best with groups of ten or fewer students. Each sheet says, "Congratulations, _____ I saw you do this positive act today: _____." Each student has to write a congratulatory statement to all the other students in the class and give it to them. This has all students focus on positive statements and lets each student see that others have seen what they have done well.

These activities are important for students because they need to learn to recognize their positive actions and develop a positive frame of mind. We want this positive thinking to become a habit so that when the students are faced with a testing situation, they can make positive statements about themselves.

One of the things that I have done, when students had gotten into trouble and we were discussing the consequences and what happened, was to make students repeat a positive statement about themselves or about what would happen the rest of the day. One day, a student had gotten himself into trouble in the morning, and after he had calmed down and received the consequence, I processed the event and ended the discussion with him by saying, "And I know you can have a good rest of the day." Then I asked him what kind of a day the rest of the day was going to be for him and he replied, "I'm gonna have a gooder rest of the day."

Stress Balls

We have discussed the use of fidgets (see Chapter 7)—stress balls, twisters, play dough, or a favorite small toy. These can all be very effective for students when taking a test. Another variation is the red rubber ball stress ball. This is one of the author's favorite activities to do prior to a test. You can purchase a happy face beach ball and write on it several stress reduction activities, such as the following.

- Plaster a smile on your face for ten seconds.
- Rub some lotion on your hands (teacher would have that available).
- Play with some play dough (teacher provides small party pack).
- Scratch your back (teacher provides a toy back scratcher).
- Tense your muscles, hold for five seconds, then relax them.
- Think of a very happy memory.
- Say to yourself, "I can do this, I can do this."
- List five things you do well.
- Blow some bubbles. (I like to get small bubble jars and give a jar to the child whose thumb lands on this one.)

Vary these according to the age of your students. The teacher then throws the ball to one student, who has to do whatever the ball says where his or her left thumb lands. The student then throws the ball to another student, and so on until all the students have engaged in a stress reduction technique. This relieves anxiety prior to a test for all the students.

Reinforcement for Working

While we cannot offer reinforcement to the student for specific answers during the test, we certainly can do so for students who begin working, who keep working during the test, and who hang in there and finish the test.

Bubble Sheet Practice

Students become more comfortable with a situation that could provoke anxiety when they have familiarity with it. They then know what they face. To prepare students to take tests, provide them with practice tests. They need the opportunity to practice using bubble sheets and taking a variety of tests. The more practice, the less stressful the tests become for the student.

Many years ago, I remember observing in a classroom in which young children were taking a test with a bubble sheet for the answers. The students had not been exposed to the use of a bubble sheet and were crying over the frustration this caused. Completing a test with bubble sheets requires several skills. The students must understand that the questions and answers are to be read on one sheet and the corresponding answer is to be marked on the bubble sheet. Students who have problems with tracking may easily lose their place in moving from the test sheet to the bubble sheet. Students with fine-motor problems may have difficulty filling in the answer on the bubble sheet because space is limited. And students who have weak memory skills may know the answer when they see it in the test booklet but may forget it when they move their eyes over to the bubble sheet.

SENSORY ADAPTATIONS DURING TESTING

During a workshop for high school teachers I conducted, they shared the story of some the high school juniors who took the state test. They observed that some students were sucking their thumbs, and the teachers couldn't figure out why they were doing that. I explained that to meet their own sensory needs, these students needed to suck on something, and all they had in the setting that was appropriate to suck on were their own thumbs. I suggested that, in the future, they might want to consider letting the students have a water bottle for the test, allow them to suck on a peppermint hard candy, or let them wrap a fruit roll-up around their pencil and suck on that (as discussed in Chapter 7).

Teachers should work with parents to ensure that on the day of tests, parents make sure that their children wear comfortable clothes so that the texture doesn't bother them. For example, tags in the backs of some students' shirts can drive them up a wall. Parents can buy tag-free clothes for children or they can cut the tags out of items.

I remember an eighteen-year-old student relaying the support that she gained from having a squeeze stress ball with her during the test. I also have encouraged students to take an item with them that is comforting, like some type of fidget.

TEACHING TEST-TAKING STRATEGIES

Test-wiseness is a term used to describe the ability of the student to use test characteristics, formats, and test-taking situations to raise test scores (Millman, Bishop, & Ebel, 1965). It is independent of the knowledge of subject matter. Teaching test-wiseness focuses on use of time, error avoidance, how to guess when you don't know the answer, deductive reasoning, and answering multiple-choice questions (Ritter & Idol-Maestas, 1986).

Lancaster, Schumaker, Lancaster, and Deshler (2009) have found that the preferred test preparation approach includes using test-taking strategies along with content instruction. A number of test-taking strategies have been developed. One such uses the acronym SCORER (Carman & Adams, 1972).

S—Schedule your time.

C—Clue words.

O—Omit difficult questions.

R—Read carefully.

E—Estimate your answer.

R—Review your work.

This strategy has not only been used with high school students, but also with students as early as sixth grade (Ritter & Idol-Maestas, 1986). The students must not only be taught the acronym but what each of the words in the acronym mean as well. Students must be thoroughly taught the steps in the strategy process and they must have plenty of opportunities for practice.

One of my favorite research-based test-taking strategies for students with learning disabilities and students with emotional and behavioral disorders is PIRATES (Hughes, Schumaker, Deshler, & Mercer, 1988).

P—**Prepare to succeed.** Students learn to write their name on their paper, allot the time that they believe will be needed, and think positive thoughts.

I—**Inspect the instructions.** Students learn to carefully read the directions and even underline key words in the directions.

R—**Read, remember, and reduce.** Students read each item carefully, think about the item, and then reduce the choices that are not likely to be correct.

A—**Answer or abandon.** Students answer questions they do know and temporarily skip items they are unsure about.

T—**Turn back.** Students return to the questions they abandoned previously.

E—**Estimate.** Students make a good guess when they are unsure about an answer.

S—**Survey.** Students then go back over the test and do any necessary clean-up.

Recently software called the *Test-Taking Strategy CD* (Lancaster, Schumaker, Lancaster, & Deshler, 2009) was developed. The program on this CD teaches the PIRATES strategy to students. A detailed description, modeling, verbal practice, and controlled practice with immediate feedback are built into the program. Research has shown that this is an effective tool for junior and senior high school students with learning disabilities, and it also can be used in a large group setting.

Carter and colleagues (2005) suggest that test-taking strategy instruction will make a more positive difference if it is also combined with content instruction and appropriate accommodations to form a comprehensive intervention package.

Focus on Direction Words

Reading and Highlighting the Direction Words

You may have adopted this mantra when you bought something that requires assembly: "When all else fails, read the directions." Unfortunately that mantra gets us into trouble on tests because, if we fail to read the directions, we may answer all the questions incorrectly. While teachers can remind students to read the directions, when students are given the test, they are busy scanning it and seeing what they know and what they don't know, tuning out the teacher who is trying to give the directions.

I am a firm believer in the use of highlighters and like to use this format for assisting students in reading the directions. Once tests are distributed to students, the teacher then reads the test directions aloud, has students read the test directions out loud together, and then has the students highlight the directions. The teacher may want to write the directions on the board and highlight them so the students are more likely to highlight the directions on their test.

Teaching the Meaning of the Direction Words

As noted in Chapter 4, a teacher of young students relayed a story to me about the importance of teaching the meaning of direction words before giving a test. Typically the students were used to direction to draw a circle around the right answer. She gave them a test one day and several students had blank looks on their faces because the directions said: "Draw a ring around the right answer." The students didn't know what that meant.

Prior to giving any test, the teacher should review it to determine the specific direction words that are present and whether some of those words might cause confusion. If there is any chance that students may not know the words, then the teacher should provide instruction and practice in those words. The teacher may want to create a cue card or a bookmark for direction words and their meanings. I know that some teachers make a bookmark with the specific direction word on it; in one column the teacher puts the words that are most commonly used in tests given at the grade level, and in the second column the teacher puts a picture depiction of the meaning of the word.

Pointing Out Changes in Directions During the Test

Chapter 4 discusses the problems with worksheets and the number of times that directions change, even on one sheet of paper. This also happens on tests as well. Halfway through the page, the directions change but the student did not notice that and completes the section incorrectly.

Prior to the test, the teacher should alert the students to any change in directions in the middle of the page and have the students highlight those directions. The teacher may have the students highlight those directions in a different color to assist them in realizing that there is a change.

Instead of using highlighters, the teacher may want to give the students small sticky notes and have them put a small sticky note by the new directions.

Focus on the Vocabulary of the Test Content

State departments of education or testing companies usually provide sample test questions from the state test that teachers can use to prepare their students. Teachers should definitely avail themselves of those sample test questions, especially to review the vocabulary words that are used within the content. The teacher should inspect those vocabulary words and make sure the students are exposed to them and have a chance to review them. The teacher can do a pretest to see how many of those vocabulary words the students already know, and then can plan activities accordingly to build vocabulary.

A Familiar Individual to Administer the Test

The individual who administers the test is an important factor in students' success. Children are likely to do better on a test when it is administered by someone with whom the student is familiar, someone who has a positive rapport with the student. The identity of the individual giving the test can make a significant difference in the child's comfort level in taking a test. The child should feel a sense of emotional support, comfort, and familiarity.

We have learned this certainly is so when working with children with autism. They do not adjust well to change, so if someone new comes into a classroom to take the student out for a test, the student automatically becomes very anxious at not knowing who the test examiner is. Prior to giving any test where the test examiner will be someone the child does not know, it is critical that the examiner establish a rapport with the student.

Case in point: I gave a test in a postsecondary situation to a young adult with whom I had a very positive rapport. She had a learning disability and it was necessary that the test be read to her. In many cases, tests were read to this young lady by another individual. However, I knew the tremendous amount of test anxiety this young lady had so I gave her a choice: the test could either be administered by the other individual or I offered to tape the test questions and she could go to a quiet area with the test itself and could put headphones on and listen to me read the questions. She quickly chose the tape recording option because she was familiar with my voice. The added benefit of this was that she could listen to the test questions several times until she fully grasped the content. She reported that hearing my voice was comforting to her and reduced her anxiety.

A Familiar and Comfortable Testing Environment

Oftentimes we associate certain environments with pleasant or unpleasant events. We won't go to a certain store because a sales clerk was rude to us. We avoid driving on a certain road because we once slid on the ice there. Students also associate school environments with good and bad events. Students may associate the principal's office with being in trouble, for instance. Some children with autism do better in environments that are familiar to them. As a result, if we take a student into a strange room and send her or him down to the principal's office to complete a test, the student may not do as well on the test as in the familiar classroom, which is hopefully a pleasant environment for the student.

It certainly is not always possible to control the setting in which a student with special needs has to take a test; however, we can prepare the student for a change in setting. As an example, if a student with autism is going to have to take the state test in a separate room because of the specific accommodations that are required, the teacher or another adult can take the student to that room a couple of weeks before the test and do a pleasant activity with the student so that the student associates the room with doing a pleasant activity. Over the course of the two weeks, the teacher may take the student to that room a few more times, again to do a pleasant activity. That way when the student has to go to the room for testing, the student is familiar with it and associates it with doing something pleasant.

A teacher I knew allowed her students to bring their house slippers on the day of the test and they could wear them during the test so that they felt more comfortable.

Chapter 6 on environmental adaptations discusses the importance of beauty in the environment. We used to think that test environments needed to be sterile ones, but now find ourselves asking why we thought so. Isn't it more pleasant to walk into a room where there is beauty—with plants, nice lighting, and carpeted areas to diffuse sound? We should work to make our test environments more homey and comfortable, and less sterile.

Test Survival Kit

Students who have organizational problems may forget to bring more than one pencil for a test, they break the tip of the pencil and become upset, or they don't have an ample eraser or scratch paper. If students come into a testing situation unprepared, they get off to a bad start. Test survival kits are a must, and they may need to vary according to the student. Students have preferences for the types of pencils they use, or if they use pencils that have a smell, then they prefer a particular scent. Some students need pencil grips and, because there are so many different types, they probably have a specific preference.

In the test survival kit, the student might prefer a particular type of fidget. A student recently reported to me that she believes that having her fidget with her during the test was what helped her to cope with the stress of the entire situation. Students will need scratch paper. They also may need highlighters, a ruler, a calculator, sticky notes, and extra erasers. The teacher can create these test survival kits or can work with students to develop their own kits that are tailored for their specific needs. Parent support can be elicited for some of the supplies. The teacher might put some of these items on the list they provide to parents at the beginning of the school year about the supplies the students need.

Periodic Breaks: Antiseptic Bouncing

When faced with difficult tasks, we work hard and are exhausted when we finish because we had to exert a great deal of mental or physical effort. The same holds true for children with special needs who are faced with a test. It is very difficult and exhausting for them, and they will need periodic breaks to regroup themselves.

Antiseptic bouncing is discussed in Chapter 5, on behavioral adaptations, and it is critical we use it during testing. Antiseptic bouncing involves giving a break to a child who is getting frustrated with a particular task. A student may get to a section of a test that he or she perceives is difficult to do. The child scowls and has the death grip on the pencil—we see the growing frustration. This is when we may want to say to the student, "Looks like your pencil needs sharpening—why don't you take it over to the pencil sharpener, sharpen it, and come back?" Or the teacher may say, "How about if you put your head down for two minutes and take a break?" You are bouncing the student out of the difficult situation and, hopefully, when upon return to the task, the student will have a more positive outlook and may continue.

Hurdle Help

Some students start working on a test, come to the third question, don't know the answer to the question, and freeze. They give up and don't go any further. As a result they don't do well on the test because they didn't complete much of it. We need to help the student over the hurdle by saying, "Looks like question number three has you stumped. How about if you go on to numbers four, five and six, and then come back and look at number three?" This teaches the student that it is okay to skip an item that might appear difficult and then to come back to it. This may get the student back on the right track. After successfully answering more questions, the student may have a more positive mind-set upon returning to the hard one and may be up to the challenge. It also may be that the next questions give the student a clue about the answer to the one that stumped them.

Prompt or Cue Cards

When preparing a student for a test, a number of cue cards can be considered. It will be important, though, that you check ahead of time to ensure that the cue card does not jeopardize the integrity of the test. The following are some ideas for what to put on cue cards.

- A test-taking strategy such as PIRATES
- Stress reduction techniques
- A proofreading checklist
- The meaning of direction words

Summary: Just 3×5 It

1. Accommodations in assessment should match accommodations in instruction.

2. Individuals who are providing testing accommodations should receive training.

3. Universal design allows text to be digitized to facilitate accommodations.

4. Ways that we can teach children how to deal with test anxiety include building positive affect.

5. Educators should provide opportunities for students to practice taking tests and practice using bubble sheets.

6. It is important to make the testing environment as comfortable as possible for students and to provide sensory adaptations.

7. Educators should focus on teaching students about following directions.

8. Test-taking strategies promote test-wiseness.

13

Homework Adaptations

W e all recognize the importance of collaboration between the teacher and the parent or guardian in the success of the student. Yet homework can serve as a major barrier in collaboration. It can in fact cause a lot of friction between the teacher and the parent and can produce a great deal of stress for the entire family. Just as we adapt student work within the classroom, we must also adapt the homework that we give to our students.

Homework should be independent work that the child can do on his or her own, and it should be an opportunity for the child to practice skills or reinforce what was learned at school. The teacher should spend some time at the end of the day reviewing the homework direction and having students do a small portion of that work at school, so there is a quick check on whether the child actually understands how to do the assignment, the work is too hard for the student, or the student can do the work independently (Margolis, 2005).

The environment in which homework is done will not be same for all students. One student may come from a home in which both parents take an active interest in the child's education, are home in the evening, and are very able to assist with homework. Another child may come from a home with many stressors, such as a mother trying to raise two children alone, trying to go to school, and working full time. One family has a very quiet home environment. Another family lives in a home where people come and go and there are usually a lot of people visiting at any given time. A teacher could innocently give a student a project to draw a picture of his or her bedroom or have the student provide the measurements of the room when the student doesn't have a bedroom—the children sleep in the living room. Some families have computers with high-speed Internet access; some families don't have a computer or, if they have one, several children and their parents have to share it. It is the role of the teacher to establish a positive relationship with the families and to get to know their specific needs.

ASSESSING THE NEEDS OF THE FAMILY

Having worked with many families over the years, I have learned that sometimes we, as educators, are quick to criticize the families; yet we did not have to cope with many of the stressors that they face. We work with children when we are fresh and alert. Parents face their children upon their return from school; the parent may have worked all day and may be tired. The parent may be dealing with the stressors of raising a family. Some single parents are raising their children and working two or three jobs to make enough money to support the family. Some parents may have had bad experiences within school themselves, which results in a bias against school personnel. Some children are being raised by grandparents who don't have as much energy as they had twenty years earlier.

How can we best determine the needs of the family? Teachers have many students and don't have the time to learn about each family. However, school personnel can try to connect with the family prior to the start of the school year by writing a letter of introduction to the parent or guardian, offering them the opportunity to meet before the school year starts. We also can talk with the student's previous teacher or the building administrator to gain as much information as possible about the family's situation.

You may also want to prepare a very short, nonintrusive questionnaire for the family that asks such questions as what the general schedule is at home in the evening, what time does the family have dinner, and what activities does the family like to do together.

SENSITIVITY TO THE NEEDS OF THE FAMILY

We must all be sensitive to the needs of the family and get to know the family as much as possible so we can provide homework that is appropriate within the framework of the home environment. We may give the students an assignment that requires computer research but the child does not have access to a computer at home. After the bus ride home, the student may arrive home at 4:30 to find the electricity has been turned off in the home, and there is no light for the child to see to do homework. We may give homework to a student who is expected to be the caregiver for young children at home while the parents work, so the student doesn't have time to do any homework. I worked with a student whose mother moved frequently and often lived with a relative, until the relative threw the family out. There were days when the student wasn't sure whether he would still be living in the same location when he got off the bus.

EVALUATING HOMEWORK

It is a good idea to periodically ask parents to evaluate the homework that you have given to their children. They are usually glad to be asked how the homework is going. Some possible questions for a homework evaluation sheet include:

- Were the directions clear?
- Was the reading too difficult?
- How long did it take your child to complete the homework assignment?
- Is there anything I could do to ensure that the child is successful in completing the homework assignment?

Responses to these questions can assist you in planning further homework.

COORDINATING HOMEWORK WITH OTHER TEACHERS

Matt and his family ended up at the emergency room one night after Matt suffered a bad asthma attack. While at the emergency room, Matt cried that he needed to get home because he had to get his homework done. Matt had entered junior high school and that evening had arrived home with four hours worth of homework to do. The English teacher gave homework, the math teacher gave homework, the science teacher gave homework, and the history teacher gave homework. Each subject required at least one hour.

As teachers, we believe that our subject area is the most important. While our subject area is important to us, we need to look at the big picture and understand the total demands that are made on students each day. Teachers need to make efforts to coordinate their homework assignments—perhaps one teacher gives a short amount of homework one night because the math teacher gives more on that night of the week. Teachers of students at the middle and secondary school level need to communicate with each other so they can judge the total amount of time that students have in homework.

HOMEWORK SURVIVAL KITS

The teacher can work together with the students to develop homework survival kits for each subject area. The survival kit can include file folders, pens, pencils, erasers, a calculator, bookmarks, paper, and whatever else may be necessary for the student to complete homework assignments.

At the beginning of the year, each night before the student goes home, the teacher should provide a checklist for what the student will need for completing the homework. The student should have to copy the checklist and make sure to have everything necessary before leaving the building. Eventually the teacher can fade out the cues, but should be teaching students how to organize themselves so they take home the right materials.

Some teachers require students to use folders with pockets in them. One pocket is labeled as an outbox, meaning that the students put the work that is to go home in it. The other pocket is labeled as input, meaning that this is where homework goes that has been completed and should be returned to the school.

Some students like to keep a three-ring binder with dividers for each class. They enjoy putting their papers in a binder. Other students don't like this approach and would rather use file folders or folders with pockets in them. The teacher will need to expose the student to a variety of ways to keep materials organized to determine what works best for that student. (See Chapter 11 for more on using file folders and binders.)

ASSIGNMENT NOTEBOOKS

It is important that students have a way to record assignments and to take that record home so the parent knows what homework is expected. From the time students are old enough to be assigned homework, they should be taught how to use an assignment notebook. Students should be exposed to differing types of calendars and assignment notebooks. More about that is discussed in Chapter 10 on timing and scheduling adaptations. The teacher should present a visual depiction of what the homework is and provide the time for the students to complete their own list. At the end of the day, the teacher can review what the homework assigned is, check to see if students have the assignments recorded, and also check to see if the students are taking the necessary materials home to complete the homework. Students should be recognized for taking the homework home, completing it, and returning it to school.

NOTEBOOKS FOR COMMUNICATION BETWEEN PARENTS AND TEACHERS

A common practice for some students with special needs is a notebook that goes between the school and the home. The parent writes down what type of morning or evening the child had at home, and the teacher records how the student has done at school and what homework may need to be completed. Teachers must be very clear in explaining what the child is supposed to do and what work must be completed by the next day. Teachers have to be realistic about how much time they actually have at the end of the day to send the parent an update. I have seen too many teachers who have agreed to send a notebook home every day with information about what the child did at school and what needs to be done when the child arrives home. The teacher then gets busy at the end of the day and doesn't have time to complete the notebook. This then discourages the parent who has been promised a note home daily. The teacher must make every effort to write something in the notebook.

The teacher also must make sure that the tone of a notebook back and forth is positive and focuses on what the student has done well that day. It is too easy for the parent to perceive that the teacher doesn't like the student if notes have a negative tone.

ALTERNATIVES TO TRADITIONAL HOMEWORK

Typically the homework assignment is a series of worksheets or specific writing assignments. This may be very stressful to the student who does not like worksheets and for the parent who is at a disadvantage without the teacher's manual to figure out what the correct answers may be. Whenever an independent practice can be made into a game, you are fostering the possibility of family enjoyment and family togetherness. Here are some examples (some of which you may recognize as classroom adaptations mentioned elsewhere in this book).

- When studying vocabulary words, the students can make a concentration game with a specified number of words. The teacher gives the students a set of index cards or sheets of paper cut into a specified number of squares. The student writes the word on one card and the definition on another card. The cards are shuffled and put facedown on the table and the family can play the game and try to match the vocabulary words to the correct definition. The same type of game can also be utilized for math facts.
- Jeopardy is a fun game to review social studies information. The teacher can write a series of answers arranged according to

categories in boxes on a piece of paper. Small sticky notes can be used to cover the answers and the sticky notes can denote the value of the answer.

- Bingo is a fun family game that can be used to review specific facts. The teacher can make the bingo cards with specific math answers and then provide a sheet with questions for the family to call out.

- Scavenger hunt games are fun for young students when the educator is working on teaching letter sounds. The teacher sends home a letter sound and children have to collect objects that begin with that letter sound. For older students, scavenger hunts can be used when working on specific vocabulary words. The students have to look around the house for magazine or newspaper articles or books that include the word. The object is to find as many of the words as possible.

- The clue game is great to play at home. The student may be reading a story or about social studies. The teacher can send home a set of clues about the story or the lesson and the parent is asked to hide the clues around the house so the student can find the answer in the text according to the clues given.

For any game, the educator may also want to consider giving the family directions so the child and the parent(s) can make their own game and come back to school and show how they created it. If the educator does not want to spend a great deal of time making games, the educator can take file folders and have students make their own board game with steps similar to Candyland and then can vary sets of questions according to the subjects.

MORE IDEAS TO INCREASE THE LIKELIHOOD THAT HOMEWORK WILL BE COMPLETED

The following are more ideas designed to increase the likelihood that homework will actually be completed by the student.

- Graphic organizers are an excellent way for a student to learn to visually organize the material given. For social studies review, the educator can provide a blank graphic organizer (after teaching the student how to use a graphic organizer). The complexity of the graphic organizer will depend on the age and maturity of the student. The student can take the graphic organizer, along with the textbook, home and complete it. Students can also be encouraged to design their own graphic organizers. A number of software programs are available to do so, but again be very careful that you don't require the student to create one if that student doesn't have access to a computer.

- Just as we want to empower students to make choices, we can and should build choices into homework assignments. When first instituting a choice system for homework, the teacher may give the students two choices. As students get used to making choices, the teacher can create a homework tic-tac-toe, with nine possible activities listed on a tic-tac-toe sheet and the student, together with the family, chooses any three activities to complete.

- Grades are certainly reinforcing for some students, but a number of students are not reinforced by them. A student may perceive getting good grades to be difficult or not worth the effort, or the student may get more attention from the teacher by not completing the assignments. The chapter on behavioral adaptations, Chapter 5, includes a number of ideas for reinforcing students' positive behavior at school—it is also important to use some of those strategies for students who complete their homework. Another additional reinforcement idea is provided next.

- Offer coupons to "get out" of doing an assignment. I have used this effectively for students and have recommended it to others for students who will not complete homework. If students complete two or three homework assignments (whatever the teacher believes is an appropriate number but the teacher should not make the number too high or the student will give up before starting), then the student earns a coupon to be excused from one homework assignment. When I shared this idea with a group of teachers at a staff development session, one teacher became incensed, saying that she would never give a student a coupon to get out of an assignment because all of the homework assignments she gave were critical. The teacher who believes this should not use this idea. But if students are not motivated to do any homework assignments and this strategy results in homework being completed, then the idea is successful.

- To assist students in studying spelling words, the parents and student can work together to write the word on one side of an index card and on the other side draw a picture or some other type of graphic to assist in remembering the word. Human billboards are also a fun activity (which is also discussed in Chapter 7). Students can make a human billboard with two pieces of poster board and string. The student writes the spelling words on both sides of the billboard, or writes the difficult words on one side of the board and a graphic depicting the word on the other. The parent can then wear the billboard around the house to help the student remember the spelling words.

Summary: Just 3×5 It

1. Educators must be cognizant of the stress that homework can put on the family and must work to ensure that homework is both appropriate and a family activity that can bring the family together in a valuable and fun learning experience.

2. It is important to remember that homework is done in differing home environments, and we should work cooperatively with families to assess their needs.

3. Educators of students at the middle and high school level should coordinate with one another about the amount of homework given.

4. Periodically, educators should ask families to complete a homework evaluation sheet.

5. Homework survival kits, assignment notebooks, and home-school notebooks are useful tools for students.

6. Alternatives to traditional homework include concentration/memory games, bingo, scavenger hunts, and clue games.

7. Ideas that increase the likelihood that homework will be completed include graphic organizers and choices.

8. It is important to recognize those students who complete homework. Coupons to get out of an assignment also may be used.

Conclusion

When I began writing this book, I wanted to make sure that I gave my readers at least 101 practical adaptations. After writing down the ideas, I quickly learned that there were many more that I would be providing. This book actually contains more than 400 adaptations. I am hoping that these ideas will have a "snowball" impact on your work and many more adaptations will come about in your classroom.

One idea can generate many more. Teachers are creative and motivated professionals—if they are given an idea they can change it, depending on the level of the students and depending on their particular circumstances. They are motivated to look for the answers they need to meet the needs of their students. It is my hope that after reading the many adaptations contained in this book, all of you will think of many other ideas that you can use to make your classroom successful for students with special needs.

Planning and implementing adaptations will not only help one student who has special needs but also may be of benefit to other students in your classroom. Adaptations pave the way for the active involvement of the students in learning.

With the many stresses facing today's teachers, I hope that you daily reflect on the positive difference you are making in the lives of your students. Commend yourself for being an educator and remain the life-long learners you are.

References

Abrams, B. (2005). Becoming a therapeutic teacher for students with emotional and behavioral disorders. *Teaching Exceptional Children, 38*(2), 40–45.

Acrey, C., Johnstone, C., & Milligan, C. (2005). Using universal design to unlock the potential for academic achievement of at-risk learners. *Teaching Exceptional Children, 38*(2), 22–31.

ADA Amendments Act of 2008. Pub. L. No. 110-325, 122 Stat. 3553 (2008).

Armendariz, F., & Umbreit, J. (1999). Using active responding to reduce disruptive behavior in a general education classroom. *Journal of Positive Behavior Interventions, 1*(3), 113–135.

Au, K. (2001). Culturally responsive instruction as a dimension of new literacies. *Reading Online, 5*(1). Retrieved March 26, 2010 from http://www.readingonline.org/new/literacies/lit_index.asp?HREF

Beck, I., McKeown, M., & Kucan, L. (2002). *Bringing words to life: Robust vocabulary instruction.* New York: Guilford.

Bolt, S., & Thurlow, M. (2004). Five of the most frequently allowed testing accommodations in state policy: Synthesis of results. *Remedial and Special Education 25*(3), 141–152.

Borgia, L., Owles, C., & Beckler, M. (2007). Terrific teaching tips. *Illinois Reading Council Journal, 35*(3), 29–32.

Brentar, J. (2008). Psychological disorders and functional limitations. *Journal of Learning Disabilities: A Multi-disciplinary Journal. 15*(3), 131–136.

Brophy, J. (1983). Classroom organization and management. *Elementary School Journal, 83,* 265–286.

Bryan, T., & Bryan, J. (1991). Positive mood and math performance. *Journal of Learning Disabilities, 24,* 490–494.

Bryan, T., Sullivan-Burstein, K. & Mathur, S. (1998). The influence of affect on social-information processing. *Journal of Learning Disabilities, 31*(5), 418–426.

Carman, R., & Adams, W. (1972). *Study skills: A student's guide for survival.* New York: John Wiley.

Carter, E., Wehby, J., Hughes, C., Johnson, S., Plank, D., Barton-Arwood, S., et al. (2005). Preparing adolescents with high-incidence disabilities for high-stakes testing with strategy instruction. *Preventing School Failure, 49*(2), 55–62.

Cartledge, G., & Kourea, L. (2008). Culturally responsive classrooms for culturally diverse students with and at risk for disabilities. *Exceptional Children, 74*(3), 351–371.

Christle, C., & Schuster, J. (2003). The effects of using response cards on student participation, academic achievement, and on-task behavior during whole-class, math instruction. *Journal of Behavioral Education, 12,* 147–165.

Connor, D., & Lagares, C. (2007). Facing high stakes in high school: 25 successful strategies from an inclusive social studies classroom. *Teaching Exceptional Children, 40*(2), 18–27.

Conroy, M., Sutherland, K., Snyder, A., Al-Hendawi, M., & Vo, A. (2009). Creating a positive classroom atmosphere: Teachers' use of effective praise and feedback. *Beyond Behavior, 18*(2), 18–26.

Czarnecki, E., Rosko, D., & Fine, E. (1998). How to CALL UP notetaking skills. *Teaching Exceptional Children, 30*(6), 14–20.

Darrow, A. (2007). Adaptations in the classroom: Accommodations and modification, part 1. *General Music Today, 20*(3), 32–34.

DeBoer, A. (1986). *The art of consulting.* Chicago: Arcturus Books.

DeBoer, A. (1995). *The art of consulting and communicating.* Longmont, CO: Sopris West.

Doe v. Withers, 20 IDELR 422 (West Va. Circuit Court, 1993).

Dreikurs, R. (1964). *Children: The challenge.* New York: Hawthorn Books.

Edgemon, E., Jablonski, B., & Lloyd, J. (2006). Large-scale assessments: A teacher's guide to making decisions about accommodations. *Teaching Exceptional Children, 38*(3), 6–11.

Fletcher, J., Francis, D., O'Malley, K., Copeland, K., Mehta, P., Caldwell, C., et al. (2009). Effects of a bundled accommodations package on high-stakes testing for middle school students with reading disabilities. *Exceptional Children, 75*(4), 447–463.

Ford, D., & Kea, C. (2009). Creating culturally responsive instruction: For students' and teachers' sakes. *Focus on Exceptional Children, 41*(9), 1–16.

Fore, C., Boon, R., & Lowrie, K. (2007). Vocabulary instruction for middle school students with learning disabilities: A comparison of 2 instructional models. *Learning Disabilities: A Contemporary Journal, 5*(2), 49–73.

Freedman, M., & Myers, J. (1952). Rock around the clock [Recorded by Bill Haley and His Comets]. On *Rock around the clock.* New York: Decca Records (1954).

Grant, K. (2009). Beyond graphic organizers: Why inspiration is a quintessential UDL tool. *Special Education Technology Practice, 11*(1), 28–37.

Greenwood, C., Hart, B., Walker, D., & Risley, T. (1994). The opportunity to respond and academic performance revisited: A behavioral theory of developmental retardation and its prevention. In R. Gardner, D. M. Sainato, J. O. Cooper, T. E. Heron, W. L. Heard, J. Eshleman, et al. (Eds.), *Behavior analysis in education: Focus on measurable superior instruction* (pp. 213–223). Pacific Grove, CA: Brooks/Cole.

Griffith, A., Trout, A., Hagaman, J., & Harper, J. (2008). Interventions to improve the literacy functioning of adolescents with emotional and/or behavior disorders: A review of the literature between 1965 and 2005. *Behavioral Disorders, 33*(3), 124–140.

Hagan-Burke, S., Burke, M., & Sugai, G. (2007). Using structural analysis and academic-based intervention for a student at risk of EBD. *Behavioral Disorders, 32*(3), 175–191.

Haydon, T., Borders, C., Embury, D., & Clarke, L. (2009). Using effective instructional delivery as a classwide management tool. *Beyond Behavior, 18*(2), 12–17.

Heward, W. L. (1996). Three low-tech strategies for increasing the frequency of active student response during group instruction. In R. Gardner III, D. M. Sainato, J. O. Cooper, T. E. Heron, W. L. Heward, J. W. Eshleman, et al. (Eds.), *Behavior analysis in education: Focus on measurably superior instruction* (pp. 283–320). Pacific Grove, CA: Brooks/Cole.

Hirsch, E. (2003). Reading comprehension requires knowledge—of words and the world: Scientific insights into the fourth grade slump and the nation's stagnant comprehension scores. *American Educator,* (Spring), 10–13, 16–22, 27–29.

Hughes, C., Schumaker, J., Deshler, D., & Mercer, C. (1988). *The test-taking strategy: Instructor's manual.* Lawrence, KS: Edge.

Individuals With Disabilities Education Improvement Act of 2004. Pub. L. No. 108–446, 118 Stat. 2647 (2004).

Jacobs, H. (2010). *Curriculum 21: Essential education for a changing world.* Alexandria, VA: ASCD.

Jenson, W., Rhode, G., & Reavis, H. (1994). *The tough kid toolbox.* Longmont, CO: Sopris West.

Johns, B. (1997). Making school a place to call home. *Reaching Today's Youth, 2*(1), 34–36.

Johns, B. (1998). Approaching the millennium for students with disabilities: Implementing IDEA 97 and its accompanying regulations. *Learning Disabilities: A Multidisciplinary Journal, 9*(3), 75–79.

Johns, B., & Carr, V. (2009). *Techniques for managing verbally and physically aggressive students.* Denver, CO: Love.

Johns, B., & Crowley, E. (2007). *Students with disabilities and general education: A desktop reference for school personnel.* Horsham, PA: LRP.

Johns, B., Crowley, E., and Guetzloe, E. (2002). *Effective curriculum for students with emotional and behavioral disorders.* Denver, CO: Love.

Johns, B., McGrath, M., & Mathur, S. (2010). *The many faces of special educators: Their unique talents in working with students with special needs and in life.* Lanham, MD: Rowman & Littlefield Education.

Kampwirth, T. (2003). *Collaborative consultation in the schools: Effective practices for students with learning and behavior problems* (2nd ed.). Upper Saddle River, NJ: Merrill Prentice Hall.

Kiger, D. (1989). Effects of music information load on a reading comprehension task. *Perceptual Motor Skills, 69,* 531–534.

Ko, M. (2007). Au's culturally responsive instruction and balanced literacy. *The International Journal of Learning, 14*(3), 19–23.

Konrad, M., Joseph, L., & Eveleigh, E. (2009). A meta-analytic review of guided notes. *Education and Treatment of Children, 32*(3), 421–444.

Lambert, M., Cartledge, G., Heward, W., & Lo, Y. (2006). Effects of response cards on disruptive behavior and academic responding during math lessons by fourth-grade urban students. *Journal of Positive Behavior Interventions, 8*(2), 88–99.

Lampi, A., Fenty, N., & Beaunae, C. (2005). Making the three Ps easier: Praise, proximity, and precorrection. *Beyond Behavior, 15*(1), 8–12.

Lancaster, P., Schumaker, J., Lancaster, S., & Deshler, D. (2009). Effects of a computerized program on use of the test-taking strategy by secondary students with disabilities. *Learning Disability Quarterly, 32*(3), 165–179.

Lapsansky, A. (1991). *Learning strategies and teaching techniques: A handbook for students, parents, and professionals.* Lockport, IL: Innovative Learning Strategies.

Lee, D. (2005). A quantitative synthesis of applied research on high probability request sequences. *Exceptionality, 13,* 141–154.

Lee, D., Belfiore, P., & Budin, S. (2008). Riding the wave: Creating a momentum of school success. *Teaching Exceptional Children, 40*(3), 65–68.

Lerner, J., & Johns, B. (2009). *Learning disabilities and related mild disabilities: Characteristics, teaching strategies, and new directions* (11th ed.). Boston: Cengage.

Liebert, R., & Morris, L. (1967). Cognitive and emotional components of test anxiety: A distinction and some initial data. *Psychological Reports, 20,* 975–978.

Margolis, H. (2005). Resolving struggling learners' homework difficulties: Working with elementary school learners and parents. *Preventing School Failure, 50*(1), 5–12.

Margolis, H., & McCabe, P. (2003). Self-efficacy: A key to improving the motivation of struggling learners. *Preventing School Failure, 47*(4), 162–169.

McKeown, M., Beck, I., Omanson, R., & Pople, M. (1985). Some effects of the nature and frequency of vocabulary instruction on the knowledge and use of words. *Reading Research Quarterly, 20,* 522–535.

McKinney, S., Chappell, S., Berry, R., & Hickman, B. (2009). An examination of the instructional practices of mathematics teachers in urban schools. *Preventing School Failure, 53*(4), 278–284.

Millman, J., Bishop, C., & Ebel, R. (1965). An analysis of test-wiseness. *Educational and Psychological Measurement, 25,* 707–726.

Morgan, M., & Moni, K. (2007). 20 ways to motivate students with disabilities using sight-vocabulary activities. *Intervention in School and Clinic, 42*(4), 229–233.

Murray, M., Baker, P., Murray-Slutsky, C., & Paris, B. (2009). Strategies for supporting the sensory-based learner. *Preventing School Failure, 53*(4), 245–251.

Niesyn, M. (2009). Strategies for success: Evidence-based instructional practices for students with emotional and behavioral disorders. *Preventing School Failure, 53*(4), 227–233.

Peterson, S., Caniglia, C., & Royster, A. (2001). Application of choice-making intervention for a student with multiply maintained problem behavior. *Focus on Autism and Other Developmental Disabilities 16*(4), 240–246.

Premack, D. (1959). Toward empirical behavior laws. *Psychological Review, 66,* 219–233.

Premack, D. (1965). Reinforcement theory. In D. Levin (Ed.), *Nebraska symposium on motivation.* Lincoln, NE: University of Nebraska.

Reinke, W., Lewis-Palmer, T., & Merrell, K. (2008). The classroom check-up: A classwide consultation model for increasing praise and decreasing disruptive behavior (pp. 123–180). *School Psychology Review, 37,* 315–332.

Ritter, S., & Idol-Maestas, L. (1986). Teaching middle school students to use a test-taking strategy. *Journal of Educational Research, 79*(6), 350–357.

Roberts, G., Torgesen, J., Boardman, A., & Scammacca, N. (2008). Evidence-based strategies for reading instruction of older students with learning disabilities. *Learning Disabilities Research and Practice, 23*(2), 63–69.

Salend, S. (2008). Determining appropriate testing accommodations: Complying with NCLB and IDEA. *Teaching Exceptional Children, 40*(4), 14–22.

Schneider, E. (1953). The use of music with the brain damaged child. In E. T. Gatton (Ed.), *Music therapy*, (pp. 95–98). Lawrence, KS: Allen Press.

Scott, V., & Compton, L. (2007). A new TRICK for the trade: A strategy for keeping an agenda book for secondary students. *Intervention in School and Clinic, 42*(5), 280–284.

Simon, P., & Woodley, B. (1966). Red rubber ball [Recorded by The Cyrkle]. On *Red rubber ball*. New York: Columbia Records.

Stormont, M., & Reinke, W. (2009). The importance of precorrective statements and behavior-specific praise and strategies to increase their use. *Beyond Behavior, 18*(3), 26–32.

Sutherland, K., Lewis-Palmer, T., Stichter, J., & Morgan, P. (2008). Examining the influence of teacher behavior and classroom context on the behavioral and academic outcomes for students with emotional or behavioral disorders. *The Journal of Special Education, 41*(4), 223–233.

Taylor, A., & Bunte, J. (1993). Rich vein of diversity yields classroom activities. *Curriculum Review, 32*(6), 20.

Tilton, L. (2005). *The teacher's toolbox for differentiating instruction*. Shorewood, MN: Covington Cove.

Turner-Vorbeck, T. (2005). Expanding multicultural education to include family diversity. *Multicultural Education, 13*(2), 6–10.

U.S. Department of Education. (2002). *No child left behind: A desktop reference*. Washington, DC: U.S. Department of Education.

Vanderbilt, A. (2005). Designed for teachers: How to implement self-monitoring in the classroom. *Beyond Behavior, 15*(1), 21–24.

Webster-Stratton, C., & Reid, M. J. (2002). An integrated approach to prevention and management of aggressive behavior problems in preschool and elementary grade students: Schools and parents collaboration. In K. Lane, F. Gresham, & T. O'Shaughnessy, T. (Eds.), *Children with or at risk for emotional and behavioral disorders* (pp. 261–278). Boston: Allyn & Bacon.

Weishaar, M., & Boyle, J. (1999). Note-taking strategies for students with disabilities. *Clearing House, 72*, 392–395.

Wilson, B., & Love, M. (1964). I get around [Recorded by The Beach Boys]. On *All summer long*. Hollywood, CA: Capitol Records.

Wright, D., & Gurman, H. (1994). *Positive interventions for serious behavior problems: Best practices implementing the Hughes Bill (A.B. 2586) and the positive behavioral intervention regulations*. Sacramento, CA: Resources in Special Education. Retrieved July 31, 2010, from http://www.pent.ca.gov/pos/cl/str/useofreinforcement.pdf

Yasutake, D., & Bryan, T. (1996). The influence of affect on achievement and behavior of students with learning disabilities. *Journal of Learning Disabilities, 28*, 329–334.

Yehle, A., & Wambold, C. (1998). An ADHD success story: Strategies for teachers and students. *Teaching Exceptional Children, 30*(6), 8–13.

Zirkel, P. (1994, April). Costly lack of accommodations. *Phi Delta Kappan*, 652–653.

Index

CORWIN
A SAGE Company

The Corwin logo—a raven striding across an open book—represents the union of courage and learning. Corwin is committed to improving education for all learners by publishing books and other professional development resources for those serving the field of PreK–12 education. By providing practical, hands-on materials, Corwin continues to carry out the promise of its motto: **"Helping Educators Do Their Work Better."**